HOLT

WORLD HISTORY

Reading Like a Historian Toolkit

HOLT, RINEHART AND WINSTON

A Harcourt Education Company

Orlando • **Austin** • New York • San Diego • London

Contents

Contributor

Sam Wineburg, Ph.D
Professor and Chair
Curriculum and Teacher Education
Professor of History (by courtesy)
Stanford University
Stanford, California

Reviewers

Steve Goldberg
NCSS Board of Directors
Social Studies Department Chair
New Rochelle High School
New Rochelle, New York

Susan Ramírez, Ph.D
Penrose Chair of History and Latin American Studies
Texas Christian University
Fort Worth, Texas

Peter Stearns, Ph.D
Professor of History and Provost
George Mason University
Fairfax, Virginia

Reading Like a Historian

For more Reading Like a Historian resources, visit

go.hrw.com
Keyword: Historian

- **Links** to approved Web sites for student research on historical topics
- **Student** Internet activities including:
  - –How to analyze an artifact
  - –How to analyze written sources
  - –How to analyze historical maps
  - –How to analyze works of art
  - –How to analyze an infographic
  - –How to analyze a photograph
  - –How to analyze a political cartoon
- **The Holt Researcher**—a database of primary and secondary sources
- **The Holt Grapher**—software that allows students to enter data and create a variety of charts and graphs
- **The World Atlas**
- **Presentation and Essay Scoring Rubrics** for the Reading Like a Historian Toolkit

Holt's Reading Like a Historian Toolkit offers practical advice for investigating and understanding historical sources. The Toolkit contains a variety of resources to help you teach your students how to read like historians, including: professional essays by history education expert Dr. Sam Wineburg, teaching strategies, student activities and transparencies, answer key and rubrics, motivational classroom poster, and links to Holt's Reading Like a Historian Web site.

What is Reading Like a Historian?

Reading like a historian is about as far from mindless memorization as you can get. Instead, it means examining what the people of the past have left behind—their diaries, letters, photographs, secret government documents, and more—and evaluating this evidence in order to come to a better understanding of our shared past.

Reading like a historian is not simply a reading strategy; it is an all-encompassing way of thinking, reading, and talking, of constant skepticism when analyzing historical documents. When reading a historical document, historians think about the author's assumptions, interpretations, biases, perspectives, and goals, looking constantly for evidence of context, bias, and purpose. Most students, on the other hand, concentrate on content and facts, and assume author objectivity when reading a document. Reading like a historian is a learned process, not a natural one, but it is only this active inquiry that truly makes history spring to life.

How to use the teaching strategies

The strategies included in the Toolkit are intended to walk you and your students through the challenging process of reading like a historian using the *cognitive apprenticeship* model. Cognitive apprenticeship is a three-part approach. First, in *teacher modeling*, the teacher models expert questioning and reading techniques by "thinking aloud" while reading a document. Second, in *guided student practice*, the teacher helps students begin to analyze documents. Finally, in *independent practice*, students read documents independently, imitating the investigative strategies modeled by the teacher. Much as a trade apprentice learns from an expert of the craft, the student-apprentice learns from the teacher-expert how to read like a historian.

The strategies included in the Toolkit will help you make the historian's thought process visible to your students. Although the strategies use certain documents and activities from the Toolkit as examples, all strategies should be used with all documents.

How to use Dr. Sam Wineburg's essays

Dr. Sam Wineburg is Professor of Education at Stanford University, where he directs the nation's only doctoral program in History Education. In the professional essays included in the Toolkit, Dr. Wineburg writes eloquently about the historical inquiry in which historians engage, explaining that historians see themselves as detectives searching for clues to a puzzle that can never be entirely solved. Dr. Wineburg's essays provide further support for the investigative techniques used in the Toolkit's teaching strategies.

How to use the student activities and transparencies

The Toolkit contains 13 document-based activities, with questions and tasks designed to help your students become better readers of historical documents. Each activity focuses on a specific time period in world history, and each includes one overhead transparency reproducing a document from that activity. You may wish to use the transparencies to walk your students through the historian's thought process—sourcing, contextualizing, evaluating, analyzing, and, above all, questioning documents.

Reading Like a Historian

Sam Wineburg

What does it mean to read like a historian? When I asked a group of 10th graders, they were stumped. "Maybe it's like having a mind that spins around like a computer, crammed with dates and facts and stuff," answered one. "Remembering everything you've ever read—you know, like a photographic memory," said another.

The truth is that historians are not computers and they have no better memories than the rest of us. While many historians know a lot about certain areas, when you ask them questions about topics and eras they haven't studied, they seem pretty much like anyone else. So, if historians are not encyclopedias, what makes them distinctive? How they read.

History as an Argument

When historians sit down to read a letter from a 16th century Spanish cleric, a novel from a 19th century Russian writer, or even a chapter from the textbook you are now holding, they approach it

as an *argument*. Not in the sense of a brawl or street fight. But in the sense of someone making a claim, stating a position, trying to convince us that his or her description of events should be believed.

When we read like a historian we notice things we've never seen before. Think about it. Compare your history textbook with those written 30 or 40 years ago, which had titles like *Rise of Western Civilization* or the *Triumph of the West* or the *Tradition of Western Society*. These older books taught students that what mattered most was what happened in the West, particularly in Europe. They drew a straight line from the Greeks and Romans to Medieval Europe to the Renaissance and the "discovery" of the New World. Now and then the four-fifths of the world's population who are not heirs to the Western tradition would make an appearance. But the message was clear. The West and its peoples were at the center. Everyone else was in the margins.

History books today make a different argument: the whole of human history, not just the West, is our *legacy*, our inheritance. Accordingly, for us to truly understand the world we need to look beyond our narrow slice of it. Ancient China is as much a part of who we are, and who we will become, as ancient Greece.

Your Role in the Argument

Once you understand history as an argument you have a crucial role to play in it. History can no longer be served on a silver platter for you to swallow whole. Once you see history as an argument you realize that for every major historical interpretation, there are multiple ways of viewing things. You can't sit back and watch this happen; you have to make up your own mind.

Reading Like a Historian

Sam Wineburg

You see, calling something an argument means that it must be defended, must be backed by evidence rather than committed unquestioningly to memory.

Consider this: the Industrial Revolution occurred in England during the years 1780 to about 1830. While historians might dicker over the precise dates of the Industrial Revolution, few dispute that something big and important took place. But the moment we turn from this fact to the question of "why"—why did the Industrial Revolution occur in England and not, for example, in China or India we've landed ourselves in the middle of a raucous argument.

On one side are the historians who claim that the key factor in the birth of the Industrial Revolution was chance and something called "contingency." According to their argument, the British were lucky enough to have vast coal deposits in their soil, which fueled the ravenous industrial machine by providing a steady

The Tree of LIBERTY...with the Devil tempting John Bull.

stream of cheap fuel. England also had a convenient source of cheap cotton and a ready market for finished textiles in her American colonies. These factors, so the argument goes, were not destined or preordained but were contingent: They happily came together at the right time and the right place to produce the Industrial Revolution. There's only one reason why China and India didn't industrialize before England, according to this reasoning. In the words of one historian: "They simply did not have colonies or coal."

Hogwash, argue historians on the other side. The Industrial Revolution that swept England "was not a matter of chance, of 'things simply coming together.'" The scientific and technological superiority of Britain, writes a historian on this side, "was itself an achievement . . . the result of work, ingenuity, imagination, and enterprise."

There you have it—you are in the midst of a historical dogfight.

© The Metropolitan Museum of Art, Rogers Fund, 1919 (19.164) Photograph © 1998 The Metropolitan Museum of Art

Sam Wineburg

Making Historical Judgments

How do you know which is right? Here's where it gets dicey. There is no single right answer to big questions of historical interpretation like there is in math. Interpretations aren't right or wrong as much as they are better and worse. Better interpretations account for more of the evidence and are able to explain more of the big picture—incorporating social, geographical, cultural, and political factors in so doing. Weaker interpretations ignore pieces of evidence or use ideology as a substitute for hard thinking.

Sometimes interpretive differences come about because historians focus on different time frames. Even though they may seem to be arguing about the same thing, one may focus on what occurred during a decade or a century—while others may try to capture what happened over millennia. These time differences are what historians call differences in scale. Where historians come down on the issue of the technological progress represented by the Industrial Revolution will depend on whether their focus is a 50 year period or a 500 year one. Scale determines not only what historians see but what they choose to look at.

Even though historians argue over the meaning of the past, they often draw on the same concepts in doing so. At the heart of almost every historical interpretation is the notion of continuity and change: the idea that the world before us is both the same and different from the one inhabited by people in the past. We see the interplay of continuity and change when we compare the world today with the world around 1500. Then, as now, most of the world's population lived on just under seven percent of the earth's 60 million square miles of land. Over the past 500 or so years, that hasn't changed much: 70% of the world still lives on the same 4.25 million square miles. But consider this change: Since 1500, the world's population has mushroomed from 350 million to 6 billion, an increase of 1700%. Most of these people are crammed into the same inhabited territory that was known to the world in 1500!

© Free Agents Limited/CORBIS

Why History Matters

Why should we care about any of this—continuity and change, scale, contingency, the role of ideas, or even how to read like a historian? We should care because our images of the past—how things got to be the way they are—guide the decisions we make in the present. If we think that the West owes its technological superiority to certain ways of thinking and a particular set of cultural institutions, our positions and policies toward others will be different than if we attribute our advantage to a set of environmental and historical factors that came together at just the right time.

Put differently, how we interpret the past shapes the reality we create in the present. Our reality in the present, in turn, gives birth to the world we'll inhabit in the future.

And nothing could possibly be more important than that!

© CORBIS

© Werner Forman Archive/
The Image Works

Teacher Modeling

STRATEGY 1: SOURCING DOCUMENTS

Overview/Purpose

In this first step of teacher modeling, you will begin to review sourcing a document with your students. Thinking is an invisible process; students often believe that expert readers can simply "get" things more quickly and easily. This modeling procedure is designed to make an expert reader's thought process visible to students.

Skills

- Reviewing Sources
- Thinking Contextually

Procedure

Using an overhead transparency (included in the Toolkit) or handouts, begin by reading the document aloud. As you read, pause to ask the preview questions below, thus modeling for the class the thought process of the expert reader. If students are unable to answer the questions, you may choose to provide answers or hints. The purpose of this strategy of reading, questioning, and answering is to provide a conceptual model of interacting with documents that students will later use on their own.

- **Who is the author? What particular beliefs or biases might the author have?** Direct students to look at the attribution line. Ask the questions: What do you know about this author? Might he or she have any particular beliefs or biases? For example, students might note that the author of Document 1 in Activity 7 is given as an African man, so he might be expected to have a negative view of European imperialism, which led to African slavery.

- **What do you already know about this topic?** Choose a document from one of the activities. Encourage students to look at the title and other clues. Ask the questions: How does this topic fit into a time and place in history? What was happening during this period? Does this reading relate to any big issues you have studied in this class?

- **Why might this document have been created?** Direct students to look again at the attribution line. Ask the questions: When was this document created? What might be some reasons why this document was created? Was it created as a private record or a public record? To what purpose might it have been put? What is the credibility of this document? What are the limitations?

STRATEGY 2: WRITING QUESTIONS AND FINDING ANSWERS

Overview/Purpose

In this step of teacher modeling, you will help students understand how to examine their prior knowledge and assumptions about a topic. Prior assumptions can be helpful in introducing students to a topic, although it is often necessary to correct or abandon them after analyzing primary source documents. This modeling procedure is designed to illustrate the way an expert reader examines his or her prior knowledge and preconceptions about a subject and analyzes and refines these preconceptions by reading the documents. It will also help highlight the kinds of prior knowledge most useful for interacting with the specific document set.

Skills

- Recognizing Prior Assumptions

Procedure

Introduce students to the topic but don't let them read the historical context introduction. For example, for Activity 1, tell them they are going to read about ancient Indian religion. Then model, listing your prior knowledge and some possible assumptions about the topic. Be sure to think aloud as you note prior knowledge and assumptions. Again for Activity 1, write on the board such statements as *India has a long and complex history, more than 80% of India's population is Hindu,* or *Hinduism is very influential in India.* Then model for students the following steps:

- **Write several questions based on your prior assumptions.** For example, you might write for Activity 1: What religions have historically been practiced in India besides Hinduism? How did India's religious history develop? What led to changes in religious practices over time? How does Hinduism shape life in India today? What effects do other religions have there?

- **Read a document aloud.** Point out to students if and how the document answered a question you had written using this technique: Continue to think aloud as you write, sharing with students your thought processes. Next to each question, write the name of the source's author and the exact phrase or sentence that proves or disproves the assumption or answers the question. Write "FALSE" next to those assumptions proven false by the text. You may also need to reword or rephrase difficult or archaic excerpts.

- **Continue reading documents aloud.** Remind students that the primary source documents may not answer all their questions.

STRATEGY 3: UNDERSTANDING PERSPECTIVE
Overview/Purpose

This modeling procedure is designed to show students how to detect and analyze the perspective of an author and identify the evidence the author uses to support his or her position. Explain that writers of primary source documents often reflect a specific position or perspective on an issue, and the documents they create may attempt to present a case or argument to support this position.

Skills

- Evaluating Opinions
- Seeking Corroboration

Procedure

Using an overhead transparency (included in the Toolkit) or handouts, begin by reading a document aloud. This strategy also works well with editorial cartoons and other visuals. As you read, pause to ask the preview questions below, thus modeling for the class the thought process of the expert reader. The purpose of this strategy of thinking aloud by reading, questioning, and answering is to provide a conceptual model of interacting with documents that students will later use on their own.

- **What do I know about the author? What background information do I know about the author's time and place?** For example, in Document 3 of Activity 8, you might comment as you read: What do I know about Thomas Jefferson and his opinions?

- **What is the structure of the author's argument? Can I state the author's position? How does he or she build the case? Does the author's argument seem to be a sound one?** For the same document, ask: What does Jefferson say about recent events in France? Does he support them?

- **What types of evidence does the author use? How could I check this evidence? Is there evidence that the author ignores?** Again for the same document, ask: What is Jefferson's opinion based on? Do his own experiences qualify him to make the judgment he did?

STRATEGY 4: WRITING QUESTIONS FOR THE AUTHOR
Overview/Purpose
In this procedure, model for students the process of analyzing a primary source document with the goal of making a list of questions to ask the author. The strategy helps students learn what kinds of questions are appropriate to ask, explore how the questions might be answered, and discover what types of evidence would support the answers. The questions you model may focus on any aspect of the document, although this strategy works especially well with context, causality, opinion, and source issues.

Skills

- Exploring Causality
- Thinking Contextually

Procedure
Begin by reading the document, such as Document 5, Activity 13, aloud. As you read, pause to write on the board questions you would like to ask the author, Fidel Castro, about the Non-Aligned Movement. Possible questions might include the following: Which countries do you feel have taken advantage of others? What specifically have they done to make you feel resentful? How would you replace the current political structure of the world, if you had the opportunity? What effect would that have?

   This approach also works well with visual documents. For example, ask students to look at Document 3, Activity 6. Model formulating questions you might want to ask the artist, such as these: What was the atmosphere like when you painted this scene this event? What feeling or mood were you hoping to capture with your painting? Why did you choose to include the specific details that you did?

   As you ask your questions, keep in mind you are modeling for the class the thought process of the historian. Share your thinking processes. Let students follow the way your mind works as it moves through text and makes connections.

Guided Student Practice

STRATEGY 5: PREVIEWING TEXT

Overview/Purpose

In this first step of guided student practice, you will preview text with your students. Following the cognitive apprenticeship model, you will ask your students to begin imitating the investigative strategies you modeled in earlier activities, with guidance from you.

Skills

- Reviewing Sources
- Thinking Contextually

Procedure

Using an overhead transparency (included in the Toolkit), begin by uncovering and reading the title of an activity, such as "Europe's Crusader Culture" (Activity 4). Ask students what questions they might ask themselves after learning the title of the activity, after giving an example or two of your own. (What do I already know about this topic? How does this topic fit into a time and place in history? What else was happening at this time? Who were the Crusaders? Where did they live? What is the geographic area being discussed?) Have students provide answers to the questions. Then read the historical context introduction or have a student volunteer read it. As you read, pause to allow volunteers to call out more preview questions and answers. Finally, read, with pauses, one of the documents, such as Document 5 in Activity 4. Again have students ask preview questions about the Franks and their perspectives, the author and his beliefs or biases, and the reasons why the document might have been created.

STRATEGY 6: THINK-PAIR-SHARE

Overview/Purpose

In this step of guided student practice, students will work with a partner to develop historical reading skills, again with input from you. The think-pair-share format, combined with a theme, allows students to practice both individual reading skills and hone their abilities to discuss the document.

Skills

- Exploring Causality

Procedure

Begin by having students discuss the different meanings of the term *causality* (the idea that one thing causes another to happen). Explain different aspects of causality, such as physical and mental states, the kinds of causes that are active in history, the difference between sole causes and contributing causes, and how causality differs from chronological order. Using an overhead transparency (included in the Toolkit) or handouts, begin by reading the title of the activity and the historical context introduction aloud. Ask students to name some historical events suggested by the title and introduction, then suggest possible causes of the events.

Have students, in pairs, choose one of the documents. Ask the pairs to analyze their document and list events and causes they find. For example, pairs examining Document 3 in Activity 11 might infer that the cause of the destruction was the horrific fighting seen during World War I. Conclude by having the pairs share their findings about events and causes with the class.

STRATEGY 7: USING GRAPHIC ORGANIZERS
Overview/Purpose
Graphic organizers can help students organize information they read in primary source documents. Visual representations are especially valuable when students read more than one document from one period or on a single subject. In this guided student practice activity, you will model for students the choice and use of graphic organizers. Students will then choose and complete their own as they read a document with a partner.

Skills

- Evaluating Opinions

Procedure
Ask students to describe various graphic organizers they have used before in this or other classes. Have volunteers draw the organizers on the board and have them explain what kinds of information each organizer can usefully illustrate. Possible suggestions may include Venn diagrams for qualities shared and not shared; word or concept maps for general details; timelines for chronology; and main idea-details, sequence, cause and effect, problem-solution, or comparison-contrast charts.

    With students, choose a document and a graphic organizer that matches the kind of information the document provides and begin to fill it out. For example, a comparison-contrast chart or Venn diagram might compare and contrast the attitudes of the authors of Documents 4 and 5 of Activity 2 about the causes of the fall of Rome. The author of Document 4 seems to focus on military causes for the fall, while the author of Document 5 describes economic and social causes. Begin by supplying a few words and phrases for the diagram. As you add your ideas to the graphic organizer, share with students your reasoning. Then encourage students to supply their own suggestions and have them explain their own additions to the class chart.

Independent Practice

STRATEGY 8: THINK-PAIR-SHARE

Overview/Purpose

In the final step of the cognitive apprenticeship model, you remove the support you have been providing to students. Students read and analyze primary source documents and complete related activities on their own.

Skills

- Recognizing Prior Assumptions
- Seeking Corroboration

Procedure

You may wish to revisit some of the strategies you modeled previously, allowing students to use the strategies on their own. For example, students can use the think-pair-share strategy to read a document of their own choosing. To ease the transition to independent reading, consider asking students to discuss a specific aspect of the document, such as what prior assumptions might the author have had or how a historian might corroborate the writer's statements. Have pairs read a document, discuss their thoughts and reactions, and share their ideas in a class discussion.

STRATEGY 9: BUILDING A HISTORICAL NARRATIVE

Overview/Purpose

Using documents to build a historical narrative gives students practice in many of the skills taught in Reading Like a Historian Toolkit.

Skills

- Thinking Contextually
- Exploring Causality

Procedure

Have students work in small groups to build a historical narrative using all the documents in one of the Reading Like a Historian Toolkit activities. Have them arrange the documents in chronological order and weave them together to tell a story. Ask students to explain why the documents are part of the story they are telling. For example, the photographs in Activity 3 contribute to the story of the development of Islamic art. For this activity, students might want to analyze such questions as: Why are the pages in Document 1 so ornately decorated? What is the book? For Documents 2 and 3, have students examine what the photographs tell us about Islamic architecture. Have groups discuss their conclusions with the class.

Sam Wineburg

Few political theorists in history are immortalized with their own adjective. But Niccolo Machiavelli has bequeathed to us "Machiavellian"—unscrupulous, lacking morals, bereft of conscience, roguish. But there was more than one side to this Italian author and statesman. How do we reconcile the autocratic Machiavelli of *The Prince* with the life-long republican and author of *The Discourses*, an extended panegyric on the virtues of liberty and the advantages of representative government? This is the puzzle of reading Machiavelli.

The Prince One way to solve it is to cast *The Prince* as satire, so over the top that we have no choice but to conclude that it means the opposite of what it says—a view held by Garrett Mattingly, longtime professor of European history at Columbia University. Mattingly drew inspiration from Spinoza, who read *The Prince* as a cautionary tale that warns us what happens when rulers forswear morality to ensure the survival of the state. Others, like the German philosopher Fichte, read *The Prince* as an anti-religious tract, a frontal assault on Christianity. Benedetto Croce, the 20th century Italian philosopher, saw in Machiavelli the humanist. For him, *The Prince* embodied the author's view of the nobility of man and contained its own moral code.

But overwhelmingly, the most common reading of Machiavelli and his famous book is the one we already know: the chilling statement of statecraft by a philosophizing sociopath. In this vein, the British philosopher and public intellectual Bertrand Russell coined the most unforgettable epithet. Russell damned *The Prince* as a "handbook for gangsters."

Misreading Machiavelli? How is it that a book that has been widely acknowledged as lucid and transparent, a "model of clear Renaissance prose," one whose own author proclaimed that he had "not ornamented this work, nor filled it with fulsome phrases" is given to so many divergent readings? What other philosopher could we imagine being defended with the words—the title of apiece appearing on the webpage of New York's Italian American society—"Machiavelli was not Machiavellian"?

In a magisterial review that appeared in the *New York Review of Books*, Sir Isaiah Berlin claimed that Machiavelli challenged a core assumption of the Western tradition—and it is this challenge, never explicitly stated in *The Prince*—that has given rise to so many misreading of the text. According to Berlin, at the heart of Western tradition is the "idea of the world and of human society as a single intelligible structure," an organic whole whose pieces with much human toil can ultimately be aligned. "It is this rock, upon which Western beliefs and lives had been founded, that Machiavelli seems, in effect, to have split open."

In Berlin's reading, Machiavelli is not saying, as many would have him, that there is a conflict between the private realm of morality and the public realm of statecraft. Rather—and this is *The Prince's* most radical point—Machiavelli claimed that the two spheres are incommensurate. They can never be reconciled. "If Machiavelli is right, this entire tradition—the central current of Western thought—is fallacious. For if his position is valid then it is impossible to concoct even the notion of a perfect society, for there exists at least two sets of virtues—let us call them the Christian and the pagan—which are not merely in practice, but in principle, incompatible."

If Berlin is right, we have misread Machiavelli because we have yet to read him correctly. *The Prince* called the bluff of the Western tradition, and it is easier to misread this book than to wrestle with the implications of its claim.

Sam Wineburg

Facing an imminent invasion from the north, the Emperor Taizu, uttered these words: "on our borders there is the constant threat of *barbarians*."

What's in a word? Barbarians. The word conjures up hordes of negative connotations: uncouth and uncivilized, crude in look and mien, lacking in refinement. In modern times, the phrase "barbarians at the gate" has been used to disparage everything from unscrupulous corporate takeovers to the proliferation of pop culture.

Barbarian comes to English by way of Latin, which borrowed the world from the original Greek. Grammatically, barbarian is an imitative, repeating the same syllable twice to create an effect similar to onomatopoeia. Linguists are unsure if the repeated "bar-bar" referred to how Greek sounded to a non-Greek speaker, or how foreign languages sounded to the citizens of Greece. What is clear is that the word originally conveyed a linguistic deficiency, and it is in this sense that it appears in Homer's *Iliad* (2:867).

By the time of Aeschylus, writing after the Persian invasions of Greece, the word had already taken on meanings familiar to us today, not merely as description of linguistic capacity but as a statement of one's overall being. Unsophisticated, childlike in understanding, illiterate, brutish—in sum, morally and intellectually inferior to the suave denizens of Athens.

Although Taizu was steeped in the Confucian tradition, he knew neither Greek nor Latin. Thus, when we examine the words he supposedly uttered to the residents of his kingdom we can rule out that he used *barbarian* to warn them of a threat.

Translations as Interpretations In fact, Chinese had specific words to designate those who massed on her borders depending on the direction of the threat: the Dongyi, from the East, the Nanman from the South, the Xiong from the West, and the Beidi from the North. In Western languages, these terms are often translated as "barbarian," but depending on the context, it is possible to render them as "stranger" or "outsider," neither of which radiates the same disdain as barbarian. There are some who suggest that translating these Chinese words as "barbarian" may have been a deliberate attempt to cast the Chinese in a negative light—as a supercilious people who regarded all non-Chinese as inferior and uncivilized.

At the same time, we cannot dispute that a certain amount of ethnocentrism is built into China's own name for itself: Zhongguo, "the Middle Kingdom" or the "Capital of all States." Both locate the nation in the center of the known universe—the heart of civilization and human accomplishment. Given that those who invaded China were often unlettered and from places whose achievements in art, philosophy, and architecture paled in comparison to China's, it's not surprising that China would view those beyond her borders as less developed and less cultured.

Whenever we encounter a source in another language—particularly one distant from the cognates of European languages—we should remember that the act of translation is never mechanical, but always involves choice and judgment. Choosing to render "barbarian" as "foreigner" or "stranger" or "outsider" is more than an aesthetic decision.

It constitutes, in itself, an act of interpretation.

Reading Like a Historian

Recognizing Prior Assumptions

Sam Wineburg

In any new situation, our assumptions, expectations, and beliefs filter what we see and shape the impressions that we form. It is important to remember this when reading Ibn Battutah's fascinating *Rihla* (or *Travels*), the account of this 14th century Muslim traveler and his journey across 73,000 miles, stretching from his native Tangier to Sub-Saharan Africa, along Africa's eastern coast to Madagascar, to India and Sri Lanka, and by some accounts reaching as far as China. A member of the Muslim nobility, literate, cultured, possessing an intrepid spirit and a boundless curiosity, Ibn Battutah set down his impressions once he returned to his native Morocco with the help of his ghost writer, Ibn Juzayy.

Adventures in Mali

Ibn Battutah's last journey, an eight-month sojourn in the kingdom of Mali and its cultural heart, Timbuktu, constitutes a remarkable historical source. According to Ross Dunn, author of *The Adventures of Ibn Battutah: A Muslim Traveler of the 14th Century*, the Mali accounts are priceless to historians because "we have no other surviving eyewitness accounts from the fourteenth-century . . . of the Empire of Mali which covered a huge part of the grasslands of West Africa. He is really the only eyewitness observer of Mali . . . at its imperial zenith."

Ibn Battutah's overall impressions of what he saw during his stay were mixed. As a devout Muslim, he was impressed with the piety he witnessed and notes with approval the Malians' "assiduity in prayer and their persistence in performing it in congregation." Likewise, he looked positively on the zeal this society showed in committing the Qur'an to memory. He describes an educational aid that modern readers, particularly your students, might find less attractive. To help the young learn the Qur'an, adults "put their children in chains if they show any backwardness in memorizing it, and they are not set free until they have it by heart."

Putting Perception in Its Place

As we analyze Ibn Battutah's descriptions, we must recognize that he is not merely reporting what he sees, but coding it -- right/wrong, pious/unholy, correct/deviant -- according to the Islam of his homeland. To him, the world was split into two halves: Dar-al-Islam, the domain of Islamic rule, an immense swath of territory that today comprises 40 countries and which in the 14th century provided a web of security and unity, and everything beyond its pale — the territories of the non-believers.

Reserved for special scorn in Muslim Mali were practices that Ibn Battutah associated with non-Muslims, such as the eating of carrion or animals – like dogs — forbidden by the Qur'an. However, what disturbed him most was this society's perceived immodesty compared to the Islamic practices he knew best: "One of their disapproved acts," he wrote, "is that their female servants and slave girls and little girls appear before men naked, with their privy parts uncovered. During Ramadan I saw many of them in this state, for it is the custom of the *farariyya* to break their fast in the house of the sultan, and each one brings his food carried by twenty or more of his slave girls, they all being naked. Another is that their women go into the sultan's presence naked and uncovered, and that his daughters go naked. On the night of 25 Ramadan I saw about two hundred slave girls bringing out food from his palace naked, having with them two of his daughters with rounded breasts having no covering upon them."

Travel logs such as Ibn Battutah's are invaluable historical documents but they by no means offer a transparent window on the past.

There is no such thing as "immaculate perception" and, in this sense we are no different from Ibn Battutah.

Reading Like a Historian

Sam Wineburg

We are not even sure about he origin of her name, Sei Shonagon, since *shonagon*, "lesser counselor," was a title for a woman reflecting her father's status, and her father was not a *shonagon*. Her book at first glance seems strewn together, random lists mixed with brief vignetters and idiosyncratic impressions. The origin of the book's title is shrouded in mist. Even today no one even knows where she's buried.

But 1000 years after Sei Shonagon's death, the *Pillow Book* remains in print. Its opening lines, "In Spring, the dawn; The sky, dyed in morning light, slowly brightens and purple clouds stretch across the mountain," are recited by millions of Japanese schoolchildren, who memorize passages in junior high. It is a work whose words have maintained their "freshness and individuality a millennium after they were first conceived," writes Columbia's Donald Keene, author of *Seeds in the Heart: Japanese Literature from Earliest Times to the Late Sixteenth Century.*

A Voice from the Past

When we first approach the *Pillow Book,* we are struck by the gap between the world of contemporary America and the court life of 10th century Imperial Japan. We can imagine few parallels between our students' instant-messengered lives and the cloistered existence of Sei Shonagon, much of it spent with other courtesans of the empress fanning themselves in dimly-lit rooms. The cultural codes that shape the *Pillow Book* seem impenetrable to anyone unstudied in Japanese culture. Comparing our modern lives to Sei Shonagon's invites anachronism and courts misunderstanding.

At the same time, the *Pillow Book* has withstood the test of time precisely because it bears the defining mark of every great writer: Voice. Across this 1000-year divide, even in translation, even in the face of cultural differences we can never fully fathom, we discern the unmistakable personality of Sei Shonagon. She's devilishly funny: "Things that look hot and uncomfortable— fat people with hair plastered on their foreheads"; she possesses an acerbic wit: "Things that are the reverse of the other: summer and winter, the feeling I have seeing a man I once loved but now don't"; she's a snoop, but one we can't help identifying with: "Things that make me happy: I'm delighted when I find that, after putting the scraps together, I can read a letter someone threw away."

Opinions and Insights

Her insights glisten. We trust her opinions, because she was familiar with Japanese court in a way we cannot be. She weaves this example into her list of "Hateful Things": "A lover who is leaving at dawn announces he has to find his fan and his paper. 'I know I put them somewhere last night,' he says. Since it is pitch dark, he gropes about the room, bumping into the furniture and muttering, 'Strange! Where on earth can they be?' Finally he discovers the objects. He thrusts the paper into the breast of his robe with a great rustling sound; then he snaps open his fan and busily fans away with it. Only now is he ready to take his leave. What charmless behavior! 'Hateful' is an understatement."

We easily visualize the scene. The hush of intimacy shattered by the clunkiness of a bumbling lover trying to locate the 10th century equivalent of car keys. He starts to use his fan not because he's hot, but because he's on automatic pilot and can think of nothing better to do. He's oblivious to everything—most of all to the woman whose bed he has just left.

In the *Pillow Book*, we confront a radically different culture and vastly different era. Both aspects ordinarily pose insuperable barriers to historical understanding. But Sei Shonagon's words are an exception. Her extraordinary talent, honesty, and above all humanity radiate from the 10th century and make us smile even today.

Reading Like a Historian

Seeking Corroboration

Sam Wineburg

Historians rely on corroboration as a key tool in establishing the credibility of a historical source. The act of crosschecking and comparing accounts, corroboration takes various forms.

Two accounts of the same event can be corroborated provided that they were written independently. Depending on the topic, written accounts also can be corroborated by archaeological or forensic evidence. Geographers can also be consulted when a historical source lays out a particular travel route or notes place markers.

The Problem of One Voice

What happens when only a single record remains from the past? This is the dilemma historians face when evaluating the credibility of the Greek historian Thucydides and his account of the Peloponnesian Wars.

But wait: surely the Peloponnesian Wars had to leave behind some archaeological evidence. True, there are scattered remains from this time period, but what's left is pretty skimpy, an inscription here or a record of payment to a general there. As one historian put it, "Thucydides is still more useful for the restoration of the inscriptions than inscription are for the correction of Thucydides."

The same goes for the other accounts of the conflict between Athens and Sparta. Both Plutarch and Diodorus Siculus chronicle the war, and both can be used to check Thucydides on certain details. But on those aspects for which we still turn to Thucydides's rich account—his description of Pericles's funeral oration, his keen insights in the motivations of its principle actors, his braided narrative on why these tragic events turned out as they did—Thucydides remains the historical source.

Internal Criticism

How, then, does a historian evaluate his or her reliability? Faced with but a single source, historians employ a way of reading known as "internal criticism." In essence, Thucydides is checked against himself. Does his account cohere? Does he contradict himself? Is he one-sided? Does he strive for objectivity or revel in his biases? Does he describe his methods so that readers can make judgments as to his trustworthiness?

Let's begin with the last question. In Thucydides's entire account of the Peloponnesian Wars not a single footnote appears; in fact the very notion of a documented claim (complete with bibliographic references) is a feature of modern, not ancient, historiography.

At the same time, Thucydides was obsessed with historical method and felt compelled to share with his readers the back-story to his account. For example, here is how he described his method of recording speeches: "While keeping as closely as possible to the general sense of the words that were actually used to make the speakers say what, in my opinion, was called for by each situation."

However, instead of reassuring us, Thucydides's disclosure here provides little comfort. As we listen to Pericles, are we hearing a paraphrase of the ruler's actual words or Thucydides's view of what Pericles should have said—the historian, in effect, acting as ventriloquist?

Reading Like a Historian

Sam Wineburg

On October 4, 1957, the USSR successfully launched an R-7 intercontinental ballistic missile that carried a 58-centimeter steel globe dubbed Sputnik. This metal ball, weighing 184 pounds, orbited the earth and punctured American pride.

The Space Race

American reaction was swift, bordering on panic. A new government agency, the National Aeronautics and Space Administration (NASA) was hastily formed, signaling a major new commitment in government support for research and development in science. Americans read commentaries like those in the Chicago Daily News, which warned that if the Russians could hurl a metal ball around the earth it wouldn't be long before a larger object, carrying a nuclear payload, had our address on it. Private citizens rushed to construct backyard bomb shelters and schools conducted air raid drills in which schoolchildren were taught to cover their eyes to protect them from the flash of a nuclear explosion.

Predictable reactions, we might say. But ask your students if they can imagine other reactions. Students may be able to come up with other ideas, but I doubt that they will chance on this one: Americans interpreted Sputnik as a crushing indictment of their schools.

Birth of a Crisis

The March 24, 1958 cover of *Life* magazine declared that there was a crisis in education. *Life* offered a damning comparison of the rigors of the Soviet system versus the Mickey Mouse, happy-go-lucky atmosphere of American schooling. The magazine profiled two students, Chicago's Stephen Lapekas and Moscow's Alexei Kutzhov. Stephen boasted that he was reading Robert Louis Stevenson's *Kidnapped*, while Alexei had already mastered English as a second language, the complete works of Shakespeare, and George Bernard Shaw.

Accompanying the main article was an essay by Sloan Wilson, author of *The Man in the Grey Flannel Suit*, itself a critique of American conformism. Wilson's piece, entitled "It's Time to Close our Carnival," pulled no punches: "The facts of the school crisis are out and in plain sight . . . A surprisingly small percentage of high school students is studying what used to be considered basic subjects . . . It is hard to deny that America's schools, which were supposed to reflect one of history's noblest dreams and to cultivate the nation's youthful minds, have degenerated into a system for coddling and entertaining the mediocre."

On the heels of this crisis Congress passed the $1 billion National Defense Education Act (NDEA) making education an issue of national security. Pouring money into math, science, and language instruction—recall the "New Math"—the NDEA represented a major shift in Federal education policy, which to that point had largely been an issue at the local and state level. At the initiative of President Eisenhower, the nation's top scientists, such as Glenn T. Seaborg, the 1951 Nobel laureate in chemistry and the discoverer of plutonium, occupied their time writing high school curriculum—this was after all an issue of national security. Overnight American schools went from being hunky-dory to being "in crisis."

Continuity and change is a major theme running throughout all of history. Much has changed since the Soviets launched Sputnik and the fallout landed on American schools. But the notion that the "schools are to blame," that they are "in crisis," perpetual crisis, remains a fixture in American rhetoric and culture—displaying a wondrous staying power that seemingly knows no time.

Reading Like a Historian

Activity 1

Reading Like a Historian

Religion in Ancient India

Part A: Using Source Materials

HISTORICAL CONTEXT Several thousand years ago, two of the world's great religions—Hinduism and Buddhism—emerged on the Indian subcontinent. As might be expected given their geographic origins, the two religions are closely related. In fact, Siddhartha Gautama, who became the Buddha, was born into a Hindu family. Despite their connections, however, the two religions are distinct and differ in significant ways.

TASK Using information from the documents and your knowledge of world history, answer the questions that follow each document in Part A. Your answers to the questions will help you write the Part B essay.

DIRECTIONS Examine the following documents and answer the short-answer questions that follow each document.

DOCUMENT 1

> The duties of Brahmins, Kshatriyas, and Vaisyas, and of Sudras . . . are distinguished according to the qualities born of nature.
>
> Tranquility, restraint of the senses, penance, purity, forgiveness, straightforwardness, also knowledge, experience, and belief in a future world, this is the natural duty of Brahmins.
>
> Valor, glory, courage, dexterity, not slinking away from battle, gifts, exercise of lordly power, this is the natural duty of Kshatriyas.
>
> Agriculture, tending cattle, trade, this is the natural duty of Vaisyas.
>
> And the natural duty of Sudras, too, consists in service.
>
> —*Bhagavad Gita*

1. What does this passage from the *Bhagavad Gita* describe?

_____

_____

2. What might the purpose or benefit of organizing society in this way have been?

_____

_____

Activity 1

DOCUMENT 2

Before You Read Siddhartha Gautama, who became the Buddha, was
Hindu by birth. His family consisted of Kshatriyas, or members of the
warrior class, and so Siddhartha enjoyed a privileged upbringing before
beginning his quest for enlightenment. How might Siddhartha's upbringing
have affected his experience of the world?

No Brahmin I, no prince,
No farmer, or aught else.
All worldly ranks I know,
But knowing go my way
as simply nobody:
Homeless, in pilgrim garb,
With shaven crown, I go
my way alone, serene.
To ask my birth is vain.

—Siddhartha Gautama, the Buddha

Piyadassi Thera, *The Buddha: His Life and Teaching* (1982)

3. What does Siddhartha mean when he says, "To ask my birth is vain"?

_____

_____

4. How might followers of the Buddha have used these words to change the society in
which they lived?

_____

_____

Activity 1

Reading Like a Historian

Religion in Ancient India

DOCUMENT 3
Statue of Siva, c. 900 AD

Before You View Hindus believe in many *devas*, or faces of the universal spirit they call Brahman. Each face of Brahman performs specific tasks in the world and possesses certain gifts. Three faces—Brahma, Siva, and Vishnu—are the most prominent in Hinduism. Siva represents the destroyer face of Brahman and is shown below. What other roles might different faces of Brahman have besides "destroyer"?

The Granger Collection, New York

5. What humanlike qualities does Siva possess?

_____

_____

6. How does the image portray Siva's superhuman qualities?

_____

_____

Name _____ Class _____ Date _____

DOCUMENT 4
Statue of Buddha, c. 500 BC

Before You View Buddhists try to follow the example of the Buddha, who
they believe achieved enlightenment. How might this view have affected
the images of the Buddha created by his followers?

The Granger Collection, New York

7. What features or qualities of the Buddha does this statue seem to emphasize?

_____

_____

8. What might this emphasis suggest about Buddhists' beliefs regarding the Buddha?

_____

_____

Activity 1

Reading Like a Historian

Religion in Ancient India

DOCUMENT 5

Before You Read The Buddha taught that neither an overly spiritual nor and overly worldly life would result in enlightenment. He taught followers that they could attain enlightenment through practicing certain behaviors that he called the Middle Path.

> Monks, these two extremes ought not to be encouraged by the recluse. What two? Sensual indulgence [overeating], which is low, vulgar, worldly, ignoble, [corrupt], and conducive [helpful] to harm; and self-mortification [fasting], which is painful, ignoble, and conducive to harm. The middle path, monks, avoiding the extremes, gives vision and knowledge and leads to calm, realization, enlightenment, and Nirvana. And what, monks, is that middle path? It is this Noble Eightfold Path, namely: right understanding, right thought, right speech, right action, right livelihood, right effort, right mindfulness, right concentration.
>
> —the Buddha, speaking to his followers, c. 589 BC

Piyadassi Thera, *The Buddha: His Life and Teaching* (1982)

9. How does the Buddha describe the experience of enlightenment and Nirvana?

   _____

   _____

10. What can be concluded from the fact that the Buddha wanted his followers to live a life of moderation instead of extremes?

    _____

    _____

Activity 1   Reading Like a Historian

Part B: Writing a Document-Based Essay

HISTORICAL CONTEXT Several thousand years ago, two of the world's great religions—Hinduism and Buddhism—emerged on the Indian subcontinent. As might be expected given their geographic origins, the two religions are closely related. In fact, Siddhartha Gautama, who became the Buddha, was born into a Hindu family. Despite their connections, however, the two religions are distinct and differ in significant ways.

TASK Using information from the documents and your knowledge of world history, write an essay in which you:

- Identify and describe at least two similarities and two differences between Hinduism and Buddhism.

- Analyze why these two religions prospered at the time they were introduced and through to the present day.

DIRECTIONS Using the information from the documents provided and your knowledge of history, write a well-organized essay that includes an introduction, a body of several paragraphs, and a conclusion. Use examples from at least *four* documents in the body of the essay. Support your response with relevant facts, examples, and details. Include additional outside information.

GUIDELINES
In your essay, be sure to:

- Address all aspects of the **Task** by accurately analyzing and interpreting at least *four* documents.

- Incorporate information from the documents in the body of the essay.

- Incorporate relevant outside information.

- Support the theme with relevant facts, examples, and details.

- Use a logical and clear plan of organization.

- Introduce the theme by establishing a framework that is beyond a simple statement of the **Task** or **Historical Context**.

- Conclude the essay with a summation of the theme.

Activity 2

Reading Like a Historian
Decline and Fall of the Roman Empire

Part A: Using Source Materials

HISTORICAL CONTEXT Some 2,000 years ago the Romans built a vast empire characterized by outstanding cultural, military, and civic achievements. Yet Rome's success stretched the empire's resources. The various ethnic groups within Roman territory were prone to conflict. The Roman Empire also faced a number of attacks from the outside.

TASK Using information from the documents and your knowledge of world history, answer the questions that follow each document in Part A. Your answers to the questions will help you write the Part B essay.

DIRECTIONS Examine the following documents and answer the short-answer questions that follow each document.

DOCUMENT 1
Hadrian's Wall, constructed 122–128

© Robert Harding World Imagery/CORBIS

1. After visiting the Roman province of Britain in 122, Emperor Hadrian ordered that this wall be constructed from coast to coast across the northern part of the island. What may have been the purpose of this structure?

_____

_____

2. What does Hadrian's Wall suggest about life on the fringes of the Roman Empire?

_____

_____

Activity 2   Reading Like a Historian

Decline and Fall of the Roman Empire

DOCUMENT 2
Statue of the Tetrarchs, c. 300

Before You View Upon becoming the Roman emperor in 284, Diocletian realized that the empire had grown too large for one person to manage. He appointed a co-emperor and two assistants, or caesars. Diocletian ruled in the East, his co-emperor in the West. This new system was called the tetrarchy, which means the "rule of four." Why might an emperor agree to share power with others?

© Werner Forman Archive/The Image Works

3. What do the details of this statue suggest about the powers and stature of the four rulers of the Roman tetrarchy?

_____

_____

4. How might the division of Rome under four rulers have helped solve its issues?

_____

_____

Activity 2   Reading Like a Historian

Decline and Fall of the Roman Empire

DOCUMENT 3

Before You Read When Diocletian became emperor, inflation was a major
problem in the Roman world. Prices for basic goods had risen to
astronomical levels. For example, a small portion of wheat that had sold
for seven or eight drachmas in the 100s could now sometimes sell for as
much as 120,000 drachmas! What effect did such outrageous prices have
on the common Roman citizen?

> For who is so hard and so devoid of human feeling that he cannot, or rather
> has not perceived, that in the commerce carried on in the markets or
> involved in the daily life of cities immoderate [extreme] prices are so
> widespread that the unbridled passion for gain is lessened neither by
> abundant supplies nor by fruitful years; so that without a doubt men who
> are busied in these affairs constantly plan to control the very winds and
> weather from the movements of the stars, and, evil that they are, they
> cannot endure the watering of the fertile fields by the rains from above
> which bring the hope of future harvests, since they reckon it their own loss
> if abundance comes through the moderation of the weather.
>
> —Diocletian, Prices Edict, 301

5. To what does Diocletian attribute the dramatic increase in prices of goods in Rome?

_____

_____

6. How might widespread inflation have contributed to the weakening and eventual fall
of the western Roman Empire?

_____

_____

Activity 2   Reading Like a Historian

Decline and Fall of the Roman Empire

DOCUMENT 4

Before You Read By the late 300s, large numbers of Goths were flooding into the Roman Empire in an attempt to escape invaders from the East. The Romans treated the Goths badly. In 378 the Goths revolted against the Romans at Adrianople. The Roman army suffered a humiliating defeat. What must it have been like for a Roman soldier at Adrianople?

> Amidst all this great tumult and confusion our infantry were exhausted by toil and danger, until at last they had neither strength left to fight, nor spirits to plan anything; their spears were broken by the frequent collisions, so that they were forced to content themselves with their drawn swords, which they thrust into the dense battalions of the enemy, disregarding their own safety, and seeing that every possibility of escape was cut off from them . . . At last one black pool of blood disfigured everything, and wherever the eye turned, it could see nothing but piled up heaps of dead, and lifeless corpses trampled on without mercy.
>
> Many illustrious men fell in this disastrous defeat . . . Scarcely one-third of the whole army escaped. Nor, except the battle of Cannae, is so destructive a slaughter recorded in our annals; though, even in the times of their prosperity, the Romans have more than once had to deplore the uncertainty of war, and have for a time succumbed to evil Fortune.
>
> —Ammianus Marcellinus, *The Roman History*, c. 380

5. In Ammianus Marcellinus's view, how does the Roman defeat at Adrianople compare to other military campaigns in Roman history?

_____

_____

6. What details from the selection indicate that the Roman army was overwhelmed by the Goths? What might this indicate about the state of the Roman army?

_____

_____

Activity 2

Reading Like a Historian

Decline and Fall of the Roman Empire

DOCUMENT 5

Before You Read Social and economic problems characterized the continued decline of the Roman Empire. In the following selection, a Roman citizen notes the effects of the increased division between the empire's rich and poor citizens. What information does the title of the work convey about its author?

> As the poor are the first to receive the burden, they are the last to obtain relief. For whenever . . . the ruling powers have thought best to take measures to help the bankrupt cities to lessen their taxes . . . we see the rich alone dividing with one another the remedy granted to all alike . . .
>
> Under such circumstances can we think ourselves undeserving of God's severe punishment when we ourselves continually so punish the poor? Can we believe that God ought not to exercise his judgment against us all, when we are constantly unjust? For where, or among what people, do these evils exist save only among the Romans? Who commit such grave acts of injustice as ours? Take the Franks, they are ignorant of this wrong; the Huns are immune to it; there is nothing of the sort among the Vandals, nothing among the Goths. For in the Gothic country the barbarians are so far from tolerating this sort of oppression that not even Romans who live among them have to bear it. Hence all the Romans in that region have but one desire, that they may never have to return to the Roman jurisdiction. It is the unanimous prayer of the Roman people in that district that they may be permitted to continue to lead their present life among the barbarians.
>
> Yet we are surprised that the Goths are not conquered by our resistance, when the Romans would rather live among them than at home.
>
> —Salvian, *On the Government of God*, c. 445

9. What does Salvian say is one effect of the inequalities between rich and poor Romans?

_____

_____

10. How does Salvian say life among the barbarians compares to life among the Romans for poor citizens?

_____

_____

Part B: Writing a Document-Based Essay

HISTORICAL CONTEXT Some 2,000 years ago the Romans built a vast empire characterized by outstanding cultural, military, and civic achievements. Yet Rome's success stretched the empire's resources. The various ethnic groups within Roman territory were prone to conflict. The Roman Empire also faced a number of attacks from the outside.

TASK Using information from the documents and your knowledge of world history, write an essay in which you:

- Identify some of the political, military, economic, and social challenges faced by the Roman Empire.

- Describe how the effects of those challenges contributed to the fall of the Western Roman Empire.

DIRECTIONS Using the information from the documents provided and your knowledge of history, write a well-organized essay that includes an introduction, a body of several paragraphs, and a conclusion. Use examples from at least *four* documents in the body of the essay. Support your response with relevant facts, examples, and details. Include additional outside information.

GUIDELINES
In your essay, be sure to:

- Address all aspects of the **Task** by accurately analyzing and interpreting at least *four* documents.

- Incorporate information from the documents in the body of the essay.

- Incorporate relevant outside information.

- Support the theme with relevant facts, examples, and details.

- Use a logical and clear plan of organization.

- Introduce the theme by establishing a framework that is beyond a simple statement of the **Task** or **Historical Context**.

- Conclude the essay with a summation of the theme.

Activity 3

Reading Like a Historian

Art of the Islamic World

Part A: Using Source Materials

HISTORICAL CONTEXT Islam is the religion based on the revelations of Allah to the prophet Muhammad. Islamic culture—including art, architecture, and literature—expresses the religion's teachings and values.

TASK Using information from the documents and your knowledge of world history, answer the questions that follow each document in Part A. Your answers to the questions will help you prepare the Part B multimedia presentation.

DIRECTIONS Examine the following documents and answer the short-answer questions that follow each document.

DOCUMENT 1
Two pages from a Qur'an manuscript, c. 1300
Illumination by Mohammad ebn Aibak, calligraphy by Ahmad ebn Sohrevardi

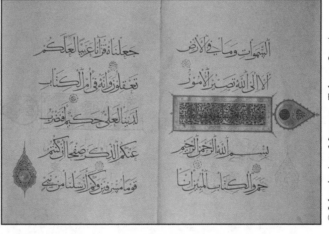

© Islamic Arts Museum, Tehran, Iran/ The Bridgeman Art Library

1. What are the major features of the art on these Qur'an pages?

   _____

   _____

2. What might the development of this art form suggest about the importance of the Qur'an to Muslims?

   _____

   _____

Activity 3

Reading Like a Historian

Art of the Islamic World

DOCUMENT 2
Window in the West Wall of the Great Mosque, Cordoba, Spain

Before You View Islam discourages the depiction of human or animal
figures in art. For this reason, much of the art produced in the Islamic
world features repeated floral patterns and geometric designs—sometimes
referred to as arabesque. For the Muslim artist, these motifs reflect beliefs
and attitudes about Allah, Islam, and the natural world. They also reflect an
interest in and knowledge of mathematics.

© Ken Welsh/The Bridgeman Art Library

3. What are the key features of the arabesque style? How does the window incorporate
these features?

_____

_____

4. How does the arabesque style reflect an appreciation for mathematics?

_____

_____

Activity 3   Reading Like a Historian
_____
                                          Art of the Islamic World

DOCUMENT 3
Minarets and Domes of the Kazimayn Mosque, Baghdad, Iraq

Before You View Islam gave rise to a distinctive form of architecture. This architecture is most spectacularly displayed in the minarets and domes of mosques—Islamic places of worship. What function do the minarets of a mosque serve?

© Chalres & Josette Lenars/CORBIS

5. Why do you think the mosque shown in this photograph is so elaborately decorated? What does this decoration suggest about the builders' feelings toward Islam?

_____

_____

6. What other Islamic art forms or styles are reflected in the image of the Kazimayn Mosque?

_____

_____

Activity 3

Reading Like a Historian

Art of the Islamic World

DOCUMENT 4

Before You Read Within Islam, a group known as the Sufis developed a special type of religious practice. Their goal was a deeper, more intense relationship with Allah. One way Sufis seek to achieve this relationship is through vivid poetry.

Your hope in my heart is the rarest treasure
Your Name on my tongue is the sweetest word
My choicest hours
Are the hours I spend with You—
O Allah, I can't live in this world
Without remembering You—
How can I endure the next world
Without seeing Your face?
I am a stranger in Your country
And lonely among Your worshippers:
This is the substance of my complaint.

—Rabi'ah al-Adawiyya, "My Greatest Need Is You," c. 740

---

7. Whom is the poet addressing in this poem? What message is the poem meant to convey?

   _____

   _____

8. How does expressing herself through poetry affect Rabi'ah al-Adawiyya's message? Explain your answer.

   _____

   _____

Activity 3

Reading Like a Historian

Art of the Islamic World

DOCUMENT 5

Before You Read Storytelling was a rich tradition in the Arab world from which Islam emerged. The following selection comes from a collection of stories featuring the exploits of a trickster named Abul-Fath al-Iskanderi, who relies on his wits to survive.

I was in Baghdad at the time of the azaz date harvest . . . My eyes fell upon a man . . . standing still with outstretched hand . . .

"Alas! I have neither two handfuls of Sawíq [porridge],
Nor melted fat mixed with flour,
Nor spacious bowl filled with Khirdíq [broth],
To soothe [my] palate,
And to remove [me] from the path of beggary.
O Giver of plenty after poverty!
Make it easy for some brave and liberal man
Of pedigree and hereditary glory,
To guide to [me] the feet of fortune
And release my life from the grip of trouble" . . .

I took from my purse a handful and gave it to him. Then he said:
"O the one who hath bestowed upon me his excellent kindness!
To God do I communicate his glorious secret,
And I pray God to keep him well-guarded,
If I have not the ability to thank him,
Then God, my Lord, will surely recompense [repay] him" . . .

So I said to him, "There is something left in the purse, therefore [show me your face] and I will give thee all." Then he removed his veil, and to by Heavens! it was . . . Abul-Fath al-Iskanderi! So I exclaimed: "Mercy on thee, how astute [clever] thou art!"

—Badí al-Zamán al-Hamdadhání, *The Maqama of the Date*, c. 975

9. Why do you think the narrator gives the man money?

_____

_____

10. How do you think this story reflects the influence of Islam?

_____

_____

Activity 3

Reading Like a Historian

Art of the Islamic World

Part B: Preparing a Multimedia Presentation

HISTORICAL CONTEXT Islam is the religion based on the revelations of Allah to the prophet Muhammad. Islamic culture—including art, architecture, and literature—expresses the religion's teachings and values.

TASK Using information from the documents and your knowledge of world history, prepare a multimedia presentation in which you:

- Identify the main forms of traditional artistic expression in the Islamic world.

- Discuss examples of how Islamic values and beliefs are expressed through art and architecture.

DIRECTIONS Using the information from the documents provided and your knowledge of history, prepare a well-organized multimedia presentation that includes an introduction, a body, and a conclusion. Use examples from at least *four* documents in the content of the presentation. Support your response with relevant facts, examples, and details. Include additional outside information.

GUIDELINES
In your presentation, be sure to:

- Address all aspects of the **Task** by accurately analyzing and interpreting at least *four* documents.

- Incorporate information from the documents into the presentation.

- Incorporate relevant outside information.

- Support the theme with relevant facts, examples, and details.

- Use a logical and clear plan of organization.

- Introduce the theme by establishing a framework that is beyond a simple statement of the **Task** or **Historical Context**.

- Conclude the presentation with a summation of the theme.

Activity 4

Reading Like a Historian

Europe's Crusader Culture

Part A: Using Source Materials

HISTORICAL CONTEXT Beginning in 1095 and lasting through 1291, Europeans launched a series of religiously based military expeditions called the Crusades. These expeditions, which originally aimed to capture Jerusalem and the surrounding Holy Land, had a significant impact on the political, economic, and social life of Europe.

TASK Using information from the documents and your knowledge of world history, answer the questions that follow each document in Part A. Your answers to the questions will help you write the Part B essay.

DIRECTIONS Examine the following documents and answer the short-answer questions that follow each document.

DOCUMENT 1

> 1. Each person will give in charity one tenth of his rents and movable goods for the taking of the land of Jerusalem; except for the arms, horses, and clothing of knights, and likewise for the horses, books, clothing, and vestments [religious garments], and church furniture of the clergy. . . .
>
> 2. Let the money be collected in every parish in the presence of the parish priest and of the rural dean . . . and of a servant of the Lord King and a clerk of the King . . . And if any one according to the knowledge of those men give less than he should, let there be elected from the parish four or six lawful men, who shall say on oath what is the quantity that he ought to have declared . . . .
>
> —Proclamation of Henry II, King of England, 1188

1. What does this passage describe?

_____

_____

2. Churches were routinely involved in collecting taxes. What other institution is involved in collecting this particular tax?

_____

_____

DOCUMENT 2
The Rise of Venice

Before You View The Crusades enhanced the power and wealth of certain European city-states. Venice, for example, became a major sea-based military power. It also became the pivot point of a flourishing trade between Europe and the Middle East, as trade goods and other valuables from the Middle East became highly prized. What besides merchandise is often exchanged when societies engage in trade?

Shelfmark# Ms. Bodl. 264, fol218r/ Bodleian Library, University of Oxford

3. What does this image suggest about Venice in the age of the Crusades?

_____

_____

4. What geographic features likely contributed to Venice's prosperity?

_____

_____

Activity 4

Reading Like a Historian

Europe's Crusader Culture

DOCUMENT 3
Advances in Military Technology

Before You View The Crusades exposed Europeans to new military techniques, technology, and architecture. For example, Europeans learned about building stone fortifications by capturing and building castles during the Crusades. As Crusaders returned from the Holy Land, castles in the far reaches of Europe began to incorporate the building styles they had used in the Holy Land.

5. The castle on the left, Krak des Chevaliers, was built in Syria between 1140 and 1260, during the Crusades. The castle on the right, Château Gaillard, was built in France in 1197. What similarities can you see between the two castles?

_____

_____

6. Why might rulers in Europe be interested in applying new, stronger building techniques to their castles?

_____

_____

Activity 4   Reading Like a Historian

DOCUMENT 4

Before You Read One profound effect of the Crusades on Western Europe
was the reduction of violent behavior in that region. This reduction in
violence took place largely because soldiers and knights found new outlets
for their aggression in fighting the Muslims, but also because popes and
rulers worked to ban violence in many lands. They sought to impose an
agreement called the Truce of God on people in Western Europe.

> From the first day of the Advent of our Lord through Epiphany [the
> Christmas season], and from the beginning of Septuagesima to the eighth
> day after Pentecost [the Easter season] and through that whole day, and
> throughout the year on every Sunday, Friday and Saturday, and on the fast
> days of the four seasons, and on the eve and the day of all the apostles, and
> on days canonically set apart—or which shall in the future be set apart—
> for fasts or feasts, this decree of peace shall be observed; so that both those
> who travel and those who remain at home may enjoy security and the most
> entire peace, so that no one may commit murder, arson, robbery or assault,
> no one may injure another with a sword, club or any kind of weapon, and
> so that no one irritated by any wrong . . . may presume to carry arms,
> shield, sword or lance, or moreover any kind of armor. On the remaining
> days indeed, viz., on Sundays, Fridays, apostles' days and the vigils of the
> apostles, and on every day set aside, or to be set aside, for fasts or feasts,
> bearing arms shall be legal, but on this condition, that no injury shall be
> done in any way to any one . . .
>
>   If a free man or noble violates [this peace], i.e., commits homicide or
> wounds any one or is at fault in any manner whatever, he shall be expelled
> from our territory, without any indulgence on account of the payment of
> money or the intercession of friends, and his heirs shall take all his
> property; if he holds a fief, the lord to whom it belongs shall receive it
> again.
>
>   —Letter from the Bishop of Cologne to the Bishop of Münster, 1083

7. What restrictions did the Bishop of Cologne place upon the people of his city?

_____

_____

8. How do you think documents like this one affected life in Europe in the Middle
   Ages?

_____

_____

Activity 4

Reading Like a Historian

Europe's Crusader Culture

DOCUMENT 5

Before You Read As a result of the contact between cultures during the Crusades, the behavior of many Europeans changed. Religious zeal drove some people to distrust and dislike Muslims and Jews, leading to many cases of violence. Other Christians, especially those who settled in the Holy Land, learned to live in peace with their non-Christian neighbors. Some of them, once labeled barbarians by the people of Constantinople and Jerusalem, adopted more genteel customs.

> Among the Franks are those who have become acclimatized and have associated long with the Muslims. These are much better than the recent comers from the Frankish lands. But they constitute the exception and cannot be treated as a rule.
>
> Here is an illustration. I dispatched one of my men to Antioch on business. There was in Antioch at that time al-Ra'is Theodoros Sophianos, to whom I was bound by mutual ties of amity [friendship]. His influence in Antioch was supreme. One day he said to my man, "I am invited by a friend of mine who is a Frank. Thou shouldst come with me so that thou mayest see their fashions." My man related the story to me in the following words:
>
> I went along with him and we came to the home of a knight who belonged to the old category of knights who came with the early expeditions of the Franks. He had been by that time stricken off the register and exempted from service, and possessed in Antioch an estate on the income of which he lived. The knight presented an excellent table, with food extraordinarily clean and delicious. Seeing me abstaining from food, he said, "Eat, be of good cheer! I never eat Frankish dishes, but I have Egyptian women cooks and never eat except their cooking. Besides, pork never enters my home." I ate.
>
> —Usmah Ibn Munqidh, *Autobiography*, c. 1175

9. What is Usmah's general attitude toward the Christians of the Holy Land?

_____

_____

10. How had life in the Holy Land changed the lifestyle of the knight Usmah's servant met?

_____

_____

Activity 4

Reading Like a Historian

Europe's Crusader Culture

Part B: Writing a Document-Based Essay

HISTORICAL CONTEXT The series of European military expeditions to the Holy Land known as the Crusades affected far more than the thousands of soldiers and civilians who fought and died in battle. The Crusades also facilitated a cultural exchange that brought great political, social, and economic change to Europe.

TASK Using information from the documents and your knowledge of world history, write an essay in which you:

- Analyze changes brought to Europe during the Crusades.

- Compare and contrast life in Europe before and after the Crusades.

DIRECTIONS Using the information from the documents provided and your knowledge of history, write a well-organized essay that includes an introduction, a body of several paragraphs, and a conclusion. Use examples from at least *four* documents in the body of the essay. Support your response with relevant facts, examples, and details. Include additional outside information.

GUIDELINES
In your essay, be sure to:

- Address all aspects of the **Task** by accurately analyzing and interpreting at least *four* documents.

- Incorporate information from the documents in the body of the essay.

- Incorporate relevant outside information.

- Support the theme with relevant facts, examples, and details.

- Use a logical and clear plan of organization.

- Introduce the theme by establishing a framework that is beyond a simple statement of the **Task** or the **Historical Context**.

- Conclude the essay with a summation of the theme.

Activity 5   Reading Like a Historian

Part A: Using Source Materials

HISTORICAL CONTEXT In 1368 a native Chinese rebellion succeeded in overthrowing the Mongol-led Yuan dynasty. Hongwu, a leader of the rebellion, became emperor and founded the Ming dynasty. Ming emperors ruled China for the next three centuries. The Ming dynasty witnessed a return to traditional Chinese values and ideals. Historians consider the period a high point in the history of Chinese arts, sciences, and government.

TASK Using information from the documents and your knowledge of world history, answer the questions that follow each document in Part A. Your answers to the questions will help you write the Part B task.

DIRECTIONS Examine the following documents and answer the short-answer questions that follow each document.

DOCUMENT 1

> The Way of Confucius was such that he was a teacher to rulers above and an educator of the people below. From the Han period to the present, no dynasty has lasted long in departure from this Way . . . My hope is to nurture gentlemen to tread in Confucius's path . . . You students must be yielding and pliant, respectful and attentive. Be resolute in matters of decorum . . . and avoid hard hotheadedness. Observe Confucius's four do-nots, and if you can cleave to what you learn as time goes by, you will be gentlemen and worthies. You will become officials of the state . . . You will bring prosperity and happiness to the people. You will make your ancestors illustrious and immortal. That is the goal.
>
> —Hongwu Emperor, lecture to Imperial University students, 1382

1. What does Hongwu believe is central to life and society in Ming China?

_____

_____

2. According to Hongwu, what will occur if the students follow the way of Confucius?

_____

_____

Activity 5

Reading Like a Historian

China during the Ming Dynasty

DOCUMENT 2
Building the Forbidden City

Before You View The home of many of the Ming emperors was the Forbidden City. The massive building project was begun in 1406 under the Yongle emperor. Its construction took 14 years to complete and required the efforts of an estimated 200,000 laborers and artisans. Once completed the palace complex covered more than 180 acres, making the Forbidden City the largest palace complex in the world.

© Free Agents Limited/CORBIS

3. What does the size and elaborateness of the Forbidden City suggest about the power of the Ming emperors?

   _____

   _____

4. What does the successful execution of such a large-scale building project indicate about the level of development of Chinese civilization under the Ming emperors?

   _____

   _____

Activity 5

Reading Like a Historian

China during the Ming Dynasty

DOCUMENT 3
Ming Dynasty Chinese Painting
Swan and Cygnets, **by Yuan-Yu Wu**

Before You View The Ming period in China is widely considered a high point of art and culture. Artists and sculptors from the period created beautiful paintings, figurines, and ceramic vessels. Despite increased contact between China and other parts of the world during the period, however, Ming artists were not much influenced by other cultures' art. Instead, the artists chose to focus on themes such as nature that had been common in Chinese art for centuries.

Yuan-Yu Wu's "Swan and Cygnets" DeAnn M. Dankowski/The Minneapolis Institute of Arts

5. What elements of this painting do you think were traditional in Chinese art?

_____

_____

6. Why do you think Ming artists wanted to continue the traditions of artists from earlier times in China's history?

_____

_____

DOCUMENT 4

Before You Read Between 1405 and 1433, the Chinese government
carried out a series of maritime expeditions under the leadership of Zheng
He. One expedition sailed as far west as the east coast of Africa. Zheng
He's voyages established Chinese authority over people throughout the
Indian Ocean area, including the people of Cochin in India. Zheng He's
voyages also spread Chinese knowledge and riches.

> How fortunate we are that the teachings of the sages of China have
> benefited us. For several years now, we have had abundant harvests in our
> country and our people have had houses to live in, have had the bounty of
> the sea to eat their fill of, and have had fabrics enough for their clothing.
> Our old are kind to the young, and our juniors respectful to their seniors;
> all lead happy lives in harmony, without the habits of oppression and
> contention for dominance. The mountains lack ferocious beasts, the
> streams are free of noxious fish, the seas yield rare and precious things, the
> forests produce good wood, and all things flourish in abundance, more than
> double what is the norm. Violent winds have not arisen, torrential rains
> have not fallen, pestilence and plagues have ceased, and there have been no
> disasters or calamities. Truly this has been brought about by the kingly
> culture.
>
> —King of Cochin submitting to Chinese rule, 1416

7. How does the king of Cochin say that Chinese rule has affected his kingdom?

   _____

   _____

8. Why do you think the king attributes the various good things he mentions to the
   Chinese?

   _____

   _____

Activity 5

Reading Like a Historian

China during the Ming Dynasty

DOCUMENT 5

Before You Read Near the end of the Ming dynasty, a scholar named Song Yingxing wrote a comprehensive work on Ming-era agriculture and technology called *The Creations of Nature and Man*. The book celebrated the practical arts and sciences at which the ordinary Chinese peasant and worker toiled. In the passage below, Song Yingxing details the state of China's coal-mining industry.

> Coal is obtainable everywhere, and is used for the smelting and calcination of metals and stones . . . There are three kinds of coal: anthracite, bituminous, and powdered . . .
>
> Of the bituminous coal, which is mostly produced in Wu and Ch'u, there are two types: the high volatile type is known as "rice coal" and is used in cooking, while the low volatile is called "iron coal" and is used in smelting and forging metals. The coal is first dampened with water before being placed in the furnace, and the bellows must be used to bring it up to red heat . . . The small fragments of this coal . . . when made into briquettes with the addition of mud and water . . . are used for cooking and . . . for smelting, calcination, and the manufacture of cinnabar.
>
> —Song Yingxing, *The Creations of Nature and Man,* 1637

9. What does this passage suggest about the state of Chinese technology and manufacturing in this era?

   _____

   _____

10. What do you think were the purposes and consequences of recording in writing this and other detailed information about China's agriculture and industry?

   _____

   _____

Activity 5   Reading Like a Historian

Part B: Preparing an Oral Presentation

HISTORICAL CONTEXT In 1368 a native Chinese rebellion succeeded in overthrowing the Mongol-led Yuan dynasty. Hongwu, a leader of the rebellion, became emperor and founded the Ming dynasty. Ming emperors ruled China for the next three centuries. The Ming dynasty witnessed a return to traditional Chinese values and ideals. Historians consider the period is high point in the history of Chinese arts, sciences, and government.

TASK Using information from the documents and your knowledge of world history, prepare an oral presentation in which you:

- Identify and describe three key achievements of the Chinese during the Ming dynasty.

- Assess the sources of Ming power and how each source contributed to the advances made in China during the period.

DIRECTIONS Using the information from the documents provided and your knowledge of history, prepare a well-organized oral presentation that includes an introduction, a body, and a conclusion. In your presentation, use examples from at least *four* documents. Support your presentation with relevant facts, examples, and details. Include additional outside information.

GUIDELINES
In your presentation, be sure to:

- Address all aspects of the **Task** by accurately analyzing and interpreting at least *four* documents.

- Incorporate information from the documents into the presentation.

- Incorporate relevant outside information.

- Support the theme with relevant facts, examples, and details.

- Use a logical and clear plan of organization.

- Introduce the theme by establishing a framework that is beyond a simple statement of the **Task** or **Historical Context**.

- Conclude the presentation with a summation of the theme.

Activity 6

Reading Like a Historian

The Northern Renaissance

Part A: Using Source Materials

HISTORICAL CONTEXT The Renaissance began and reached its peak in
Italy. By the 1400s, however, it had spread to the rest of Europe. The
Northern Renaissance, as the movement outside of Italy came to be called,
included some features that made it a distinct movement.

TASK Using information from the documents and your knowledge of
world history, answer the questions that follow each document in Part A.
Your answers to the questions will help you write the Part B essay.

DIRECTIONS Examine the following documents and answer the short-
answer questions that follow each document.

DOCUMENT 1

> Or what should I say of them that hug themselves with their counterfeit
> pardons; that have measured purgatory by an hourglass, and can without
> the least mistake demonstrate its ages . . . as it were in a mathematical
> table? Or what of those who, having confidence in certain magical charms
> and short prayers invented by some pious imposter, either for his soul's
> health or profit's sake, promise to themselves everything: wealth, honor,
> pleasure, plenty, good health, long life, lively old age, and the next place to
> Christ in the other world . . . ?
>
>   And now suppose some merchant, soldier, or judge, out of so many
> [crimes], parts with some small piece of money. He straight conceives all
> that sink of his whole life quite cleansed . . . so many treacheries bought
> off . . . and so bought off that they may begin upon a new score.
>
>   —Erasmus, *The Praise of Folly*, 1509

1. Before and during the 1500s the Catholic Church issued documents called
   indulgences that were believed to reduce the punishment people would face for their
   sins, often in return for favors or gifts. What is Erasmus's view of that practice?

   _____

   _____

2. What link does Erasmus make between magical charms and short prayers? Why?

   _____

   _____

Activity 6

Reading Like a Historian

The Northern Renaissance

DOCUMENT 2
The Marriage of Giovanni Arnolfini and Giovanna Cenami
Painting by Jan van Eyck, 1434

Before You View Art of the Northern Renaissance placed a special emphasis on achieving a high degree of realism—made possible in part with the aid of recently developed oil paints. In addition to intricate and realistic details, the painting below also incorporates the innovative Renaissance technique of perspective.

© National Gallery Collection; By kind permission of the Trustees of the National Gallery, London/CORBIS

3. What features of this painting give it such realism?

_____

_____

4. The mirror in the center of the painting shows the backs of the subjects and two other figures (presumably the painter and a witness to the ceremony). What does this feature suggest about the artist's purpose in painting the piece?

_____

_____

Activity 6

Reading Like a Historian
The Northern Renaissance

DOCUMENT 3
The Harvesters
Painting by Pieter Brueghel, 1565

Before You View Pieter Brueghel the Elder was a celebrated painter of the Northern Renaissance. He was noted for his landscapes, for his portrayal of peasant life, and for his exploration of human shortcomings.

The Metropolitan Museum of Art, Rogers Fund, 1919 (19.164)
Photograph © 1998 The Metropolitan Museum of Art

5. The subject matter of this painting—ordinary village life—was new to art in Brueghel's time. What does the painter's belief that this subject was worthy of exploration suggest about the era?

_____

_____

6. What does Brueghel's presentation of the natural world suggest to you?

_____

_____

DOCUMENT 4

Before You Read François Rabelais was a monk and physician of
Renaissance France. His great literary work *Gargantua and Pantagruel* is
known for earthy humor that poked fun at many of the institutions of the
day, including the church. Here, however, one of his main characters
celebrates the spirit of learning that swept Europe during the Renaissance.

> Now all the disciplines have been restored, languages revived: Greek,
> without which it is shameful for a person to call himself learned. Hebrew,
> Chaldean, and Latin. Elegant and correct printed editions are available, the
> result of a divinely inspired invention of my time . . . The world is full of
> learned men, fine teachers, ample libraries; and it is my opinion that
> neither in the time of Plato, nor of Cicero, nor of Papinian were there such
> opportunities for study as we see today; and no one should now go out in
> public who has not been well polished in Minerva's workshop
> [scholarship]. I see the robbers, hangmen, freebooters [pirates] and grooms
> [stable hands] of today more learned than the theologians and preachers of
> my day.
>
> —François Rabelais, *Gargantua and Pantagruel*, 1532–1542

7. What is the speaker's attitude about the availability of knowledge and learning?

_____

_____

8. What is the implication of the statement, "I see the robbers, hangmen, freebooters and
grooms of today more learned than the theologians and preachers of my day"?

_____

_____

Activity 6

Reading Like a Historian

The Northern Renaissance

DOCUMENT 5

Before You Read Literature of the Northern Renaissance often featured sharp critiques of the ideas and beliefs of the past. In one of the era's most famous works, Spanish writer Miguel de Cervantes explores and mocks the medieval notion of chivalry, or the nobleness of battle.

> At this point they came in sight of thirty or forty windmills that are on that plain.
>
> "Fortune," said Don Quixote to his squire, as soon as he had seen them, "is arranging matters for us better than we could have hoped. Look there, friend Sancho Panza, where thirty or more monstrous giants rise up, all of whom I mean to engage in battle and slay, and with whose spoils we shall begin to make our fortunes. For this is righteous warfare, and it is God's good service to sweep so evil a breed from off the face of the earth."
>
> "What giants?" said Sancho Panza.
>
> "Those you see there," answered his master, "with the long arms, and some have them nearly two leagues long."
>
> "Look, your worship," said Sancho. "What we see there are not giants but windmills, and what seem to be their arms are the vanes that turned by the wind make the millstone go."
>
> "It is easy to see," replied Don Quixote, "that you are not used to this business of adventures. Those are giants, and if you are afraid, away with you out of here and betake yourself to prayer, while I engage them in fierce and unequal combat."
>
> —Miguel de Cervantes, *Don Quixote*, 1605

9. What is Don Quixote's motivation for attacking the windmills?

   _____

   _____

10. What do you think the author is saying about Don Quixote's motives—and about chivalry in general?

    _____

    _____

Part B: Writing a Document-Based Essay

HISTORICAL CONTEXT The Renaissance began and reached its peak in Italy. By the 1400s, however, it had spread to the rest of Europe. The Northern Renaissance, as the movement outside of Italy came to be called, included some features that made it a distinct movement.

TASK Using information from the documents and your knowledge of world history, write an essay in which you:

- Identify three key features of the Northern Renaissance.

- Analyze what these features indicate about changes taking place in Europe at that time.

DIRECTIONS Using the information from the documents provided and your knowledge of history, write a well-organized essay that includes an introduction, a body of several paragraphs, and a conclusion. Use examples from at least *four* documents in the body of the essay. Support your response with relevant facts, examples, and details. Include additional outside information.

GUIDELINES
In your essay, be sure to:

- Address all aspects of the **Task** by accurately analyzing and interpreting at least *four* documents.

- Incorporate information from the documents in the body of the essay.

- Incorporate relevant outside information.

- Support the theme with relevant facts, examples, and details.

- Use a logical and clear plan of organization.

- Introduce the theme by establishing a framework that is beyond a simple statement of the **Task** or **Historical Context**.

- Conclude the essay with a summation of the theme.

Activity 7   # Reading Like a Historian

Effects of the Voyages of Discovery

Part A: Using Source Materials

HISTORICAL CONTEXT In the 1400s Europeans began sending ships into unknown waters and exploring distant lands. These voyages had profound effects on the peoples of Africa, Asia, and the Americas.

TASK Using information from the documents and your knowledge of world history, answer the questions that follow each document in Part A. Your answers to the questions will help you prepare the Part B multimedia presentation.

DIRECTIONS Examine the following documents and answer the short-answer questions that follow each document.

DOCUMENT 1

> Generally when the grown people in the neighborhood were gone far in the fields to labor, the children assembled together in some of the neighboring premises to play; and commonly some of us used to get up a tree to look out for any assailant, or kidnapper, that might come upon us—for they sometimes took those opportunities of our parents' absence, to attack and carry off as many as they could seize . . . Alas! ere long it was my fate to be thus attacked, and to be carried off, when none of the grown people were nigh. One day, when all our people were gone out to their works as usual, and only I and my dear sister were left to mind the house, two men and a woman got over our walls, and in a moment seized us both, and . . . stopped our mouths, and ran off with us into the nearest wood.
>
> —Olaudah Equiano, from *The Life of Olaudah Equiano, or Gustavus Vassa the African,* 1789

1. What is described in the above passage?

_____

_____

2. This kidnapping was typical of the way in which slaves were obtained for the slave trade. What do you think was the effect of this trade on African societies?

_____

_____

Activity 7   Reading Like a Historian

Effects of the Voyages of Discovery

DOCUMENT 2

Before You Read In 1498 Portuguese sailor Vasco da Gama rounded the southern tip of Africa and eventually reached India. This voyage opened a new trade route to Asia and gave Europe a foothold on the continent that would soon lead to widespread colonial domination. Here, Portugal's king informs his fellow European monarchs of da Gama's voyage.

> Very high, most excellent Princes and most powerful lords. Your Highnesses know how we had sent out to discover. Vasco da Gama . . . with four ships through the ocean, who had been gone for about two years now; and as the principal purpose of this enterprise for our predecessors had always been the service of God and our profit, He in His Mercy decided to bring it about according to a message that we have had from one of the captains who has not returned to us in this city, so that India and other neighboring Kingdoms . . . have been found and discovered; and they entered and navigated [India's] sea in which they found great cities and great edifices and rivers and great settlements, in which is conducted all the trade in spices and stones that passes in ships, which the same discoverers saw in great quantities, and of great size, to [Mecca], and from there to Cairo, from where it spreads out throughout the world.
>
> —Letter from Portugal's King Manuel, July 1499

3. According to the letter, what were the two purposes for da Gama's voyage?

   _____

   _____

4. What effect do you think the Portuguese discovery of Indian trade had on both countries?

   _____

   _____

Activity 7

Reading Like a Historian

Effects of the Voyages of Discovery

DOCUMENT 3

Before You Read The Spanish, who were the first Europeans to reach the Americas in the 1500s, quickly conquered the native people they found. Among those conquered were the mighty Inca, whose empire covered a large area of South America. Here, an Inca leader recalls the disruptive effect of the Spanish arrival in their empire in 1532 and how the Spanish skillfully took advantage of the resulting conflict to conquer his people.

> When my uncle Atahuallpa [the Inca emperor] saw that my father [a rival] had sent messengers and so much gold and silver to the Spaniards, he was very upset. Not only was it not lost on him how quickly he [my father] had aligned himself with them and that they recognized him as the legitimate king and lord, but also he thought that this alliance would be his doom. As he was harboring suspicion and fear of being thus cornered, he decided to summon all his people and captains who were with him in order to apprise them of the sad condition in which he found himself.
>
> —Recollection of Titu Cusi Yupanqui, 1570

5. What events is Titu Cusi Yupanqui recalling?

_____

_____

6. How do you think division among the Inca might have helped the Spanish to conquer them?

_____

_____

Activity 7   Reading Like a Historian

Effects of the Voyages of Discovery

DOCUMENT 4

Before You Read When Europeans arrived in the Americas, they spread
diseases for which the native people had no natural defenses. In the
decades following first contact, smallpox and other diseases ravaged
Native American peoples. Here, a Native American of the Pacific
Northwest recalls tales of the effects of one epidemic.

> A dreadful skin disease, loathsome to look upon, broke out upon all alike.
> None were spared. Men, women, and children sickened, took the disease
> and died in agony by hundreds, so that when the spring arrived and fresh
> food was procurable, there was scarcely a person left of all their numbers
> to get it. Camp after camp, village after village, was left desolate. The
> remains of which, said the old man, in answer by my queries on this, are
> found today in the old camp sites or midden-heaps [trash piles] over which
> the forest has been growing for so many generations.
>
> —Oral history of Squamish people,
> recorded by ethnographer Charles Hill-Tout, 1890s

7. What were the short-term effects of the epidemic described in this passage?

_____

_____

8. What do you think may have been the long-term effects of this sort of epidemic on
   this group and others across North America?

_____

_____

Activity 7

Reading Like a Historian

Effects of the Voyages of Discovery

DOCUMENT 5
The Arrival of the Horse

Before You View Europeans introduced the horse to North America. The Native Americans living on the Great Plains quickly learned to make use of the animal. How do you think the introduction of the horse might have altered the balance of life among Native American peoples?

© Smithsonian American Art Museum, Washington, DC / Art Resource

9. How are the Native Americans shown using horses?

_____

_____

10. How might the introduction of the horse have affected the lives of various groups of Native Americans?

_____

_____

Activity 7   ## Reading Like a Historian

Effects of the Voyages of Discovery

Part B: Preparing a Multimedia Presentation

HISTORICAL CONTEXT The European desire for conquest, wealth, and glory that began in the 1400s changed much of the world. As European explorers ventured to the East and West, they altered the course of history in the far corners of the world.

TASK Using information from the documents and your knowledge of world history, prepare a multimedia presentation in which you:

- Identify the places directly influenced by European exploration in the 1400s and 1500s.

- Analyze the ways in which contact with Europeans transformed the histories of people in Africa, Asia, and the Americas.

DIRECTIONS Using the information from the documents provided and your knowledge of history, prepare a well-organized multimedia presentation that includes an introduction, a body, and a conclusion. Use examples from at least *four* documents in the content of the presentation. Support your response with relevant facts, examples, and details. Include additional outside information.

GUIDELINES
In your presentation, be sure to:

- Address all aspects of the **Task** by accurately analyzing and interpreting at least *four* documents.

- Incorporate information from the documents in the presentation.

- Incorporate relevant outside information.

- Support the theme with relevant facts, examples, and details.

- Use a logical and clear plan of organization.

- Introduce the theme by establishing a framework that is beyond a simple statement of the **Task** or **Historical Context**.

- Conclude the presentation with a summation of the theme.

Activity 8

Reading Like a Historian
The French Revolution

Part A: Using Source Materials

HISTORICAL CONTEXT The French Revolution shook France to its foundation. It also sent shock waves throughout the world. The world watched anxiously as events unfolded.

TASK Using information from the documents and your knowledge of world history, answer the questions that follow each document in Part A. Your answers to the questions will help you write the Part B essay.

DIRECTIONS Examine the following documents and answer the questions that follow each document.

DOCUMENT 1
Engraving portraying the execution of Louis XVI

©Courtesy of the Warden Scholars of New College, Oxford/Bridgeman Art Library

1. The words at the top of the engraving describe the guillotine as "that instrument of French refinement." What does the artist's comment suggest?

   _____

   _____

2. Is the portrayal of the dead king meant to suggest sympathy for him? Why or why not?

   _____

   _____

DOCUMENT 2

Before You View This 1798 engraving uses the image from the Bible of a serpent tempting Eve with forbidden fruit. Here, however, the serpent is a major British supporter of the French Revolution, and the person being tempted—unsuccessfully—is John Bull, a symbol of Great Britain. What is the significance of the label that appears on the hat at the top of the tree?

The Tree of LIBERTY, with the Devil tempting John Bull.

©Courtesy of the Warden Scholars of New College, Oxford/Bridgeman Art Library

3. What do the tree and its apples represent? How can you tell?

_____

_____

4. What is the significance of the condition of the tree and its apples?

_____

_____

Activity 8

Reading Like a Historian

The French Revolution

DOCUMENT 3

Before You Read This passage addresses some of the events of the Terror. What unique perspective does the author bring to his view of the French Revolution?

> In the struggle which was necessary, many guilty persons fell without the forms of trial, and with them some innocent. This I deplore as much as anybody, and shall deplore some of them to the day of my death. But I deplore them as I should have done had they fallen in battle. It was necessary to use the arm of the people, a machine not quite so blind as balls and bombs, but blind to a certain degree. A few of their cordial friends met at their hands, the fate of enemies. But time and truth will rescue and embalm their memories, while their posterity will be enjoying that very liberty for which they would never have hesitated to offer up their lives.
>
> —Thomas Jefferson, letter to William Short, January 3, 1793

Thomas Jefferson Papers, Library of Congress, Series 1, Reel 17

5. What do you think Jefferson means when he writes, "But I deplore them as I should have done had they fallen in battle"?

   _____

   _____

6. According to Jefferson, what justifies the deaths of the innocent victims of the Terror?

   _____

   _____

Activity 8

Reading Like a Historian

The French Revolution

DOCUMENT 4

Before You Read The writer of this passage was Percy Bysshe Shelley, a British poet who possessed a strong belief in revolutionary democracy. How would you expect this belief to color Shelley's view of the French Revolution?

> If the Revolution had been in every respect prosperous, then misrule and superstition would lose half their claims to our abhorrence, as fetters which the captive can unlock with the slightest motion of his fingers, and which do not eat with poisonous rust into the soul. The revulsion occasioned by the atrocities of the demagogues, and the re-establishment of successive tyrannies in France, was terrible, and felt in the remotest corner of the civili[z]ed world. Could they listen to the plea of reason who had groaned under the calamities of a social state according to the provisions of which one man riots in luxury whilst another famishes for want of bread? Can he who the day before was a trampled slave suddenly become liberal-minded, forbearing and independent?
>
> —Percy Bysshe Shelley, in preface to his poem *The Revolt of Islam,* 1817

—Percy Bysshe Shelley, *The Complete Poetical Works* (Boston: Houghton Mifflin), 1901

7. Summarize the words, "If the Revolution had been in every respect prosperous, then misrule and superstition would lose half their claims to our abhorrence."

_____

_____

8. To what does Shelley attribute the violent excesses of the French Revolution?

_____

_____

Activity 8

Reading Like a Historian
The French Revolution

DOCUMENT 5
Engraving entitled "Promised Horrors of the French Invasion"

Before You View This 1796 engraving reflected the fear of some in Great Britain of war with revolutionary France—represented by the soldiers on the left. In the center are major British political rivals of the day. What symbols can you see that allude to the French Revolution?

©Courtesy of the Warden Scholars of New College, Oxford/Bridgeman Art Library

9. Why do you think one of the British rivals is whipping the other?

   _____

   _____

10. Describe your perception of the artist's vision of a Great Britain under French control.

    _____

    _____

Part B: Writing a Document-Based Essay

HISTORICAL CONTEXT The horrors of the Terror and the reign of Napoleon that followed made a deep impression on observers in Europe and beyond. Some celebrated the spread of the more noble ideas of the Revolution, such as liberty and equality. Others feared the breakdown of old systems of government and domination by Napoleon.

TASK Using information from the documents and your knowledge of world history, write an essay in which you:

- Describe some of the varying viewpoints on the French Revolution expressed by observers outside France.

- Discuss how and why the French Revolution represented different things to different people.

DIRECTIONS Using the information from the documents provided and your knowledge of world history, write a well-organized essay that includes an introduction, a body of several paragraphs, and a conclusion. Use examples from at least four documents in the body of the essay. Support your response with relevant facts, examples, and details. Include additional outside information.

GUIDELINES
In your essay, be sure to:

- Address all aspects of the **Task** by accurately analyzing and interpreting at least *four* documents.

- Incorporate information from the documents in the body of the essay.

- Incorporate relevant outside information.

- Support the theme with relevant facts, examples, and details.

- Use a logical and clear plan of organization.

- Introduce the theme by establishing a framework that is beyond a simple statement of the **Task** or **Historical Context**.

- Conclude the essay with a summation of the theme.

Activity 9   Reading Like a Historian
The Enlightenment Changes Views of Government

Part A: Using Source Materials

HISTORICAL CONTEXT The Enlightenment was an intellectual movement that challenged longstanding European ideas about the relationship of ordinary people to their governments. Over time, Enlightenment ideas spread beyond Europe and led to change in governments around the world.

TASK Using information from the documents and your knowledge of world history, answer the questions that follow each document in Part A. Your answers to the questions will help you write the Part B essay.

DIRECTIONS Examine the following documents and answer the short-answer questions that follow each document.

DOCUMENT 1

> We mean by natural law certain rules of justice and equity [equality], which natural reason alone has established among men, or to put it better, which God has engraved in our hearts.
>
> Such are the fundamental precepts [rules] of law and of all justice: to live honestly, to offend no one, and to render unto every man what belongs to him. From these general precepts are derived many other particular rules, which nature alone, that is to say reason and equity, suggests to men.
>
> This natural law, based as it is on such essential principles, is perpetual and unvarying: neither law nor custom can contravene [break] it . . .
>
> —Diderot and d'Alembert, *Encyclopedia*, 1751–1777

1. Where do the authors say natural law comes from?

_____

_____

2. Based on this passage, did the authors support the concept of absolute monarchy?

_____

_____

Activity 9

Reading Like a Historian

The Enlightenment Changes Views of Government

DOCUMENT 2

Before You Read Among the people who were influenced by
Enlightenment ideas was Russia's monarch, Catherine the Great. While she
did not give up her absolute power—and in fact ruled in much the manner
of the all-powerful monarchs of the past—she did express many
Enlightenment ideals in this address to her country's assembly. How does
Catherine define monarchy?

---

13. What is the true End of Monarchy? Not to deprive People of their
natural Liberty; but to correct their Actions, in order to attain the *supreme
Good* . . .

15. The Intention and the End of Monarchy, is the Glory of the Citizens of
the State, and of the Sovereign.

16. But, from this Glory, a Sense of Liberty arises in a People governed by
a Monarch; which may produce in these States as much Energy in
transacting the most important Affairs, and may contribute as much to the
Happiness of the Subjects, as even Liberty itself . . .

34. The Equality of the Citizens consists in this: that they should all be
subject to the same Laws.

35. This Equality requires Institutions so well adapted, as to prevent the
Rich from oppressing those who are not so wealthy as themselves . . .

—Catherine the Great, address to Russian assembly, 1767

---

3. What, according to Catherine the Great, is the goal of monarchy?

_____

_____

4. What does Catherine the Great say can protect the desires and freedoms of ordinary
citizens?

_____

_____

Activity 9   Reading Like a Historian

The Enlightenment Changes Views of Government

DOCUMENT 3

Before You Read The ideals of freedom and equality spread by the
Enlightenment crossed the Atlantic. In the 1800s Simón Bolívar led a
series of independence movements that challenged the rule of the Spanish.
Here he speaks to the legislature in the newly established nation of Bolivia,
the country that bears his name. What fears does Bolívar express about
forming a country?

> Legislators! As I offer you this draft of a constitution for Bolivia, I am
> overwhelmed by confusion and trepidation [fear], knowing that I have no
> talent for making laws. When I consider that the wisdom of all the ages is
> insufficient [not enough] to compose a fundamental code of law that is
> perfect, and that the most enlightened legislator can be the direct cause of
> human wretchedness . . . what can I say of the soldier, born among slaves
> and entombed [buried] in the deserts of his country, whose political
> experience is limited to the sight of captives in chains and their fellow
> soldiers taking up arms to set them free? I, a legislator? It would be hard to
> say which is more foolish, your delusion or my acquiescence [acceptance].
> I don't know who will suffer more in this horrible conflict: you, for the
> harm you should fear concerning the laws you requested of me, or I, for the
> opprobrium [criticism] to which your trust condemns me.
>
> —Simon Bolivar, address of May 25, 1826

5. What does Bolívar seem to be concerned about in this passage?

   _____

   _____

6. What do his comments suggest about his views on the proper role of government?

   _____

   _____

Name _____ Class _____ Date _____

Activity 9   Reading Like a Historian

The Enlightenment Changes Views of Government

DOCUMENT 4
A Declaration of Equality

Before You View In the French Caribbean colony of Haiti, oppressed inhabitants under the leadership of Toussaint L'Ouverture successfully rebelled against enslavement by European masters. L'Ouverture drew on Enlightenment ideas to inspire his followers. How did freedom affect life in Haiti?

© The Granger Collection, New York

7. The text in the banner at the top of the image reads "the rights of man." The caption below the image reads "liberty for the colonists." How are the ideas of rights and liberty illustrated in this image?

_____

_____

8. Why do you think the artist included a man's jacket, sword, and rifle in this image?

_____

_____

Original content copyright © by Holt, Rinehart and Winston. Additions and changes to the original content are the responsibility of the instructor.

52   Reading Like a Historian

Activity 9   Reading Like a Historian

The Enlightenment Changes Views of Government

DOCUMENT 5
A Liberty Pole

Before You View The Enlightenment extended to the American colonies and was a major influence on the growing spirit of independence that resulted in the American Revolution. Colonists put up what were known as "liberty poles" in towns and villages throughout the colonies. The liberty poles quickly became a symbol of the Enlightenment spirit and also served practical purposes. Flags raised on them summoned colonists to meetings to plan for the impending Revolution.

Library of Congress #LC-USZ62-807

9. Liberty poles, like the one pictured in this image, became a symbol of the American Revolution. What appears to be happening in this picture?

_____

_____

10. How would you characterize the event shown? What does this suggest about the ideas and feelings people had about their government during the American Revolution?

_____

_____

Activity 9   Reading Like a Historian

The Enlightenment Changes Views of Government

Part B: Writing a Document-Based Essay

HISTORICAL CONTEXT The Enlightenment was an intellectual movement that challenged longstanding European ideas about the relationship of ordinary people to their governments. Over time, Enlightenment ideas spread beyond Europe and led to change in governments around the world.

TASK Using information from the documents and your knowledge of world history, write an essay in which you:

• Identify the major political ideas of the Enlightenment.

• Analyze the ways in which these ideas influenced politics and political movements beyond Europe.

DIRECTIONS Using the information from the documents provided and your knowledge of history, write a well-organized essay that includes an introduction, a body of several paragraphs, and a conclusion. Use examples from at least four documents in the body of the essay. Support your response with relevant facts, examples, and details. Include additional outside information.

GUIDELINES
In your essay, be sure to:

• Address all aspects of the **Task** by accurately analyzing and interpreting at least *four* documents.

• Incorporate information from the documents in the body of the essay.

• Incorporate relevant outside information.

• Support the theme with relevant facts, examples, and details.

• Use a logical and clear plan of organization.

• Introduce the theme by establishing a framework that is beyond a simple statement of the **Task** or the **Historical Context**.

• Conclude the essay with a summation of the theme.

Activity 10   Reading Like a Historian
The Effects of Imperialism on Subject Peoples

Part A: Using Source Materials

HISTORICAL CONTEXT Aggressive imperialism by the United States
and European countries in the 1800s and early 1900s had a profound
impact on the peoples of Africa, Asia, and Latin America. Imperialism
brought new economic, social, and political philosophies to these regions
and changed the lives of people living there.

TASK Using information from the documents and your knowledge of
world history, answer the questions that follow each document in Part A.
Your answers to the questions will help you write the Part B essay.

DIRECTIONS Examine the following documents and answer the short-
answer questions that follow each document.

DOCUMENT 1

> At each place there is a little village, very melancholy to look at, consisting
> of hotels . . . and the small shops of the diamond dealers. Everything is
> made of corrugated iron and the whole is very mean to the eye . . . There is
> not a blade of grass in the place, and I seemed to breathe dust rather than
> air . . . The dry dusty ground, which looked so parched and ugly that one
> was driven to think that it had never yet rained in those parts, were dug in
> all directions pits and walls and roadways, from which and by means of
> which the dry dusty soil is taken out to some place where it is washed and
> the debris examined. Carts are going hither and thither, each with a couple
> of horses, and Kafirs . . . are working for 10s [shillings] a week.
>
> —Anthony Trollope, "The Diamond Fields of South Africa," 1870

1. How does Trollope say that diamond mining has affected the environment?

   _____

   _____

2. How do you think the discovery of diamonds in South Africa changed the lives of
   British colonists? How do you think it affected the African people living there?

   _____

   _____

Activity 10

Reading Like a Historian
The Effects of Imperialism on Subject Peoples

DOCUMENT 2

Before You Read European imperialism in China in the 1800s inspired the creation of a group of anti-imperialist activists known to Westerners as the Boxers. United by their resentment of what they saw as foreign interference in China, the Boxers led a bloody uprising in the late 1800s and early 1900s. The so-called Boxer Rebellion was part of a growing nationalism in China.

Late in July a proclamation of the Governor was posted in the city in which occurred the words "Exterminate foreigners, kill devils." Native Christians must leave the church or pay the penalty with their lives. Li Yü and I talked long and earnestly over plans for saving the lives of our beloved missionaries. "You must not stay here waiting for death," we said. Yet we realized how difficult it would be to escape. Foreigners with light hair and fair faces are not easily disguised. Then where could they go? Eastward toward the coast was all in tumult. Perhaps the provinces to the south were just as bad . . . So Li Yü and I went to talk the matter over with Mr. Han, the former helper, and a Deacon Wang. Both of these men had recanted [given up Christianity], but they still loved their foreign friends.

—Fei Ch'i Hao, Recollection of the Boxer Rebellion, 1900

---

3. Why does Fei Ch'i-hao say that he and his friends needed help to escape China?

_____

_____

4. Why might the Boxers have protested the presence of missionaries and other Christians in China?

_____

_____

Activity 10   Reading Like a Historian

The Effects of Imperialism on Subject Peoples

DOCUMENT 3
A Commentary on American Imperialism

Before You View Many people in Europe and the United States defended imperialism. They believed that imperialist nations were performing a service by improving the lives of people in less developed countries. The cartoon below illustrates one American newspaper's attitudes toward American involvement in the Caribbean and the Pacific.

© American History 102, Collection #2714/
Wisconsin Historical Society

5. According to this political cartoon, how did the arrival of the United States in the Caribbean and the Pacific change the lives of people there?

   _____

   _____

6. Who does this cartoon suggest benefited most from American imperialist activity? Do you think this is an accurate suggestion?

   _____

   _____

Activity 10   Reading Like a Historian

The Effects of Imperialism on Subject Peoples

DOCUMENT 4
Mohandas Gandhi and His Spinning Wheel

Before You View By the early 1900s, the British colonial rulers of India faced a growing tide of nationalism led by figures such as Mohandas K. Gandhi. Among the actions that Gandhi protested was the closing of Indian textile mills, which had led to widespread unemployment. Gandhi called on Indians to boycott European fabric and make their own on spinning wheels like the one seen in this photo.

© Margaret Bourke-White/Time & Life Pictures/Getty Images

7. Gandhi taught Indians to be proud of their heritage. How does this picture of Gandhi convey that message?

   _____

   _____

8. Why do you think Gandhi considered the spinning wheel a symbol of Indian nationalism and independence?

   _____

   _____

Activity 10   Reading Like a Historian

The Effects of Imperialism on Subject Peoples

DOCUMENT 5

Before You Read Sometimes European imperial powers disrupted existing relationships between native groups or redrew borders that had long helped keep the peace. In some cases, the effects of these changes took decades to reveal themselves. For example, this newspaper article cites imperialism as one cause for horrific violence in Rwanda in the 1990s, in which hundreds of thousands of Tutsi people were murdered by Hutu attackers in just a few months.

Ethnic tension in Rwanda is nothing new. There have always been disagreements between the majority Hutus and minority Tutsis, but the animosity between them has grown substantially since the colonial period.

The two ethnic groups are actually very similar—they speak the same language, inhabit the same areas, and follow the same traditions.

But when the Belgian colonists arrived in 1916, they saw the two groups as distinct . . . The Belgians considered the Tutsis as superior to the Hutus. Not surprisingly, the Tutsis welcomed this idea, and for the next 20 years they enjoyed better jobs and educational opportunities than their neighbors.

Resentment among the Hutus gradually built up, culminating in a series of riots in 1959 . . . When Belgium relinquished power and granted Rwanda independence in 1962, the Hutus took their place. Over subsequent decades, the Tutsis were portrayed as the scapegoats for every crisis.

—"Rwanda: How the Genocide Happened,"
BBC news report, April 1, 2004

---

9. According to this article, how did colonialism affect Hutu-Tutsi relations?

_____

_____

10. Why do you think it took so many years for the violence to surface?

_____

_____

Activity 10   Reading Like a Historian

The Effects of Imperialism on Subject Peoples

Part B: Writing a Document-Based Essay

HISTORICAL CONTEXT Aggressive imperialism by the United States and European countries in the 1800s and early 1900s had a profound impact on the peoples of Africa, Asia, and Latin America. Imperialism brought new economic, social, and political philosophies to these regions and changed the lives of people living there.

TASK Using information from the documents and your knowledge of world history, write an essay in which you:

- Identify some of the effects of colonialism in the 1800s and 1900s on the peoples of Africa, Asia, and the Americas.

- Analyze how opinions about imperialism differed among the various peoples involved.

DIRECTIONS Using the information from the documents provided and your knowledge of history, write a well-organized essay that includes an introduction, a body of several paragraphs, and a conclusion. Use examples from at least *four* documents in the body of the essay. Support your response with relevant facts, examples, and details. Include additional outside information.

GUIDELINES
In your essay, be sure to:

- Address all aspects of the **Task** by accurately analyzing and interpreting at least *four* documents.

- Incorporate information from the documents in the body of the essay.

- Incorporate relevant outside information.

- Support the theme with relevant facts, examples, and details.

- Use a logical and clear plan of organization.

- Introduce the theme by establishing a framework that is beyond a simple statement of the **Task** or the **Historical Context**.

- Conclude the essay with a summation of the theme.

Activity 11   Reading Like a Historian

The High Cost of World War I

Part A: Using Source Materials

HISTORICAL CONTEXT World War I began in 1914 and raged for more than four years. The bloodshed, destruction, and sheer horror of the war far surpassed anything the world had yet experienced.

TASK Using information from the documents and your knowledge of world history, answer the questions that follow each document in Part A. Your answers to the questions will help you write the Part B essay.

DIRECTIONS Examine the following documents and answer the short-answer questions that follow each document.

DOCUMENT 1

Paris, September 4, 1914

The following declaration has this morning been signed at the Foreign Office at London: —"The undersigned duly authorized thereto by their respective Governments hereby declare as follows:—

"The British, French, and Russian Governments mutually engage not to conclude peace separately during the present war. The three Governments agree that when terms of peace come to be discussed, no one of the Allies will demand terms of peace without the previous agreement of each of the other Allies."

—Triple Entente Declaration of No Separate Peace, September 4, 1914

1. Why do you think the Allies were interested in ensuring that none of their partners would form a separate peace with the enemy?

   _____

   _____

2. How might the war have been different if the Germans and their allies had been able to produce a separate peace with one or more of the Allies?

   _____

   _____

Activity 11   Reading Like a Historian

The High Cost of World War I

DOCUMENT 2

Before You Read Soldiers at war had long fought from entrenched
positions. In World War I, however, the digging of trenches reached a new
level of complexity. Early in the war a vast line of trenches stretched
across the whole western front, and neither side seemed capable of
breaking through the line.

> The soil is soft clay, admirably suited for entrenching, tunneling, and mine
> warfare—when it is dry. As an outside observer, I do not see why the war
> in this area should not go on for a hundred years, without any decisive
> result. What is happening now is precisely what happened last year. The
> only difference is that the trenches are deeper, dug-outs better made,
> tunnels are longer, and the charges of explosives heavier.
>
> Everywhere there are trenches, barbed wire, machine guns where they
> are least expected, and all the complicated arrangements for defense.
> Trenches are very deep, very narrow, and very wet . . .
>
> The guns are always at work. On my day of my visit to this area there
> was an almost constant bombardment going on.
>
> —Robert Donald, *Daily Chronicle*, August 1915

3. According to this passage, how have the opposing armies responded to the increased
   size and effectiveness of the trench defenses?

   _____

   _____

4. Why do you think the author of this passage says, "I do not see why the war in this
   area should not go on for a hundred years"?

   _____

   _____

Activity 11

Reading Like a Historian

The High Cost of World War I

DOCUMENT 3
Artillery Changes the Nature of Fighting

Before You View Although artillery itself was not new, World War I saw great advances in the technology. In addition to the new, more powerful guns, the ability of industry and railroads to keep armies supplied and firing—and to put thousands more troops on the battlefields—helped increase their destructive capabilities.

© Bettmann/CORBIS

5. What does the photo suggest about the ability of artillery to cause damage to people and positions?

_____

_____

6. Artillery barrages were often used against heavily defended positions, such as trenches. Based on this picture, what kind of defense could stand up to such a barrage?

_____

_____

Activity 11   Reading Like a Historian

The High Cost of World War I

DOCUMENT 4

Before You Read As the stalemate of trench warfare set in along the western front, increasingly desperate commanders turned to new ways to break through. These new methods pushed the bounds of old rules of warfare—and added to the horror of the life of a World War I soldier.

> The gaseous vapor which the Germans used against the French divisions near Ypres last Thursday, contrary to the rules of The Hague Convention, introduces a new element into warfare. The attack of last Thursday evening was preceded by the rising of a cloud of vapor, greenish gray and iridescent. That vapor settled to the ground like a swamp mist and drifted toward the French trenches on a brisk wind. Its effect on the French was a violent nausea and faintness, followed by an utter collapse. It is believed that the Germans, who charged in behind the vapor, met no resistance at all, the French at their front being virtually paralyzed.
>
> —New York *Tribune* report, April 27, 1915

7. What do you think is the significance of the statement that the use of the gas was "contrary to the rules of The Hague Convention"?

   _____

   _____

8. What is the significance of one army's choice to break a previously understood code of conduct in warfare?

   _____

   _____

Activity 11   Reading Like a Historian

The High Cost of World War I

DOCUMENT 5
New Technlogy Changes the Battlefield

Before You View In addition to improvements in artillery and the introduction of poison gas, World War I battlefields saw the introduction of several new or vastly improved types of killing machines. These devices took advantage of new scientific developments of the time. And although the success of these machines in World War I was spotty, they did help transform the battlefield into a highly efficient killing zone.

© Bettmann/CORBIS

9. What features of this device—the tank—would be useful on the battlefield of World War I?

   _____

   _____

10. How do you think the armies of World War I responded to the appearance of the tank?

   _____

   _____

Part B: Writing a Document-Based Essay

HISTORICAL CONTEXT The European quest for conquest, wealth, and glory that began in the 1400s changed much of the world. As European explorers ventured out to the east and west, they altered the course of history in many corners of the world.

TASK Using information from the documents and your knowledge of world history, write an essay in which you:

- Identify some of the unique features of the World War I political landscape and battlefield.

- Analyze how those features contributed to the unprecedented level of death and destruction.

DIRECTIONS Using the information from the documents provided and your knowledge of history, write a well-organized essay that includes an introduction, a body of several paragraphs, and a conclusion. Use examples from at least four documents in the body of the essay. Support your response with relevant facts, examples, and details. Include additional outside information.

GUIDELINES
In your essay, be sure to:

- Address all aspects of the **Task** by accurately analyzing and interpreting at least *four* documents.

- Incorporate information from the documents in the body of the essay.

- Incorporate relevant outside information.

- Support the theme with relevant facts, examples, and details.

- Use a logical and clear plan of organization.

- Introduce the theme by establishing a framework that is beyond a simple statement of the **Task** or **Historical Context**.

- Conclude the essay with a summation of the theme.

Activity 12

Reading Like a Historian

How Did the Postwar Era Affect Population Groups?

Part A: Using Source Materials

HISTORICAL CONTEXT World War II left much of Europe in ruins and disrupted and displaced millions. Some populations, such as Europe's Jews, had been devastated. Even after the war, disruption, dislocation, and relocation faced many people and groups.

TASK Using information from the documents and your knowledge of world history, answer the questions that follow each document in Part A. Your answers to the questions will help you write the Part B essay.

DIRECTIONS Examine the following documents and answer the short-answer questions that follow each document.

DOCUMENT 1

> In the first years following the end of the Nazi domination of Europe, the Gypsy [Roma] community was in disarray. The small educational and cultural organizations that had existed before 1939 had been destroyed. The family structure was broken with the death of the older people—the guardians of the traditions. While in the [concentration] camps, the Gypsies had been unable to keep up their customs . . . They solved the psychological problems by not speaking about the time in the camps. Only a small number of Gypsies could read or write, so they could not tell their own story. But also they were unwilling to tell their own stories to others, and few others were interested anyway.
>
> —Donald Kenrick and Grattan Puxon, *Gypsies under the Swastika,* 1995

1. The Roma—sometimes referred to as Gypsies—were a group that suffered severe Nazi persecution. According to this passage, how did it affect the survivors?

_____

_____

2. What about the Roma culture made the experience of the Nazi persecution so destructive to the Roma?

_____

_____

Activity 12   Reading Like a Historian

How Did the Postwar Era Affect Population Groups?

DOCUMENT 2

Before You Read The Holocaust did not create the movement to establish
a Jewish state in the ancient land of Israel, but it did give the movement
new momentum. After the war many Jews who survived picked up what
was left of their lives and answered the call to build a new life—and a new
nation.

> The catastrophe which recently befell the Jewish people—the massacre of
> millions of Jews in Europe—was another clear demonstration of the
> urgency of solving the problem of its homelessness by re-establishing in
> Eretz-Israel the Jewish State, which would open the gates of the homeland
> wide to every Jew and confer upon the Jewish people the status of a fully
> privileged member of the comity of nations.
>
> Survivors of the Nazi holocaust in Europe, as well as Jews from other parts
> of the world, continued to migrate to Eretz-Israel, undaunted by
> difficulties, restrictions and dangers, and never ceased to assert their right
> to a life of dignity, freedom and honest toil in their national homeland.
>
> —David Ben Gurion, *Declaration of Independence of Israel,*
> May 14, 1948

3. What do you think David Ben Gurion means when he refers to the "difficulties,
   restrictions and dangers" involved with the migration of European Jews to Israel?

   _____

   _____

4. How would you expect the establishment of Israel to affect the lives of Jews living in
   Europe at that time?

   _____

   _____

Activity 12   Reading Like a Historian

How Did the Postwar Era Affect Population Groups?

DOCUMENT 3

Before You Read The proposed Jewish state of Israel was to be in
Palestine, a land that had been under British control since World War I.
The Arabs who also lived on this land did not welcome the establishment
of a Jewish state on land that they thought should belong to them.
Nevertheless, the newly created United Nations lent its support to the plan.

> Independent Arab and Jewish States . . . shall come into existence in
> Palestine two months after the evacuation of the armed forces of [Great
> Britain] has been completed . . .
>
> Palestinian citizens residing in Palestine outside the City of Jerusalem, as
> well as Arabs and Jews who, not holding Palestinian citizenship, reside in
> Palestine outside the City of Jerusalem shall, upon the recognition of
> independence [of Palestine from British control], become citizens of the
> State in which they are resident and enjoy full civil and political rights.
> Persons over the age eighteen years may opt, within one year from the date
> of the recognition of independence of the State in which they reside, for
> citizenship of the other State, providing that no Arab residing in the area of
> the proposed Arab State shall have the right to opt for citizenship in the
> proposed Jewish State and no Jew residing in the proposed Jewish State
> shall have the right to opt for citizenship in the proposed Arab State.
>
> —United Nations General AssemblyResolution 181,
> November 29, 1947

5. Based on this document, how did the drive to create a Jewish state affect Palestine?

_____

_____

6. How do you think the people of Palestine might feel about the details of this
   agreement?

_____

_____

Activity 12   Reading Like a Historian

How Did the Postwar Era Affect Population Groups?

DOCUMENT 4
German Relocation after World War II

Before You View Before World War II the presence of Germans in
Eastern European countries such as Czechoslovakia and Poland had been
one of the arguments used by Germany to justify its aggressions against
those countries. After the war the Allies agreed that these Germans living
outside Germany would be relocated. This relocation often took the form
of the violent and traumatic dislocation of millions of people in Eastern
Europe.

© Bettmann/CORBIS

7. What does this photograph suggest about the circumstances under which the Germans
   were expelled from their homes?

   _____

   _____

8. How do you think forced relocation might have affected the people involved?

   _____

   _____

Activity 12   Reading Like a Historian

How Did the Postwar Era Affect Population Groups?

DOCUMENT 5

Before You Read At the end of the fighting in the Pacific, the United
States and the Soviet Union occupied the Korean Peninsula. As the Cold
War developed in the postwar period, the country of Korea was partitioned,
or divided into two halves, with each of these increasingly bitter rivals
controlling one half. The effect on the Korean people was significant.

We speak to you with the common voice of the 30 million Korean people.
To be sure, different parties have sprung up in Korea since the surrender of
our common enemy and there are differences of opinion among us. But
that is only normal in the development of democracy . . .

The most serious blunder of partitioning Korea in two occupied zones was
not of our making. It was imposed upon us . . . We say to you: We have
been divided by forces outside ourselves, like a body cut in half. How can
such a sundered body survive and function properly? We must be allowed
to have an opportunity to organize our national life as a unified whole.

—Syngman Rhee, address to the Four Allied Powers, November 4, 1945

---

9. Why is Syngman Rhee upset about the partitioning of his country?

   _____

   _____

10. What effects does he foresee on Korea as a result of the partitioning?

   _____

   _____

Activity 12   Reading Like a Historian

How Did the Postwar Era Affect Population Groups?

Part B: Writing a Document-Based Essay

HISTORICAL CONTEXT World War II was itself enormously destructive and disruptive for people in many parts of the world. It also set in motion changes that would impact populations long after the end of the war.

TASK Using information from the documents and your knowledge of world history, write an essay in which you:

- Identify some of the groups who faced challenging adjustments or difficult conditions in the years following the war.

- Analyze how the war continued to affect people long after its conclusion.

DIRECTIONS Using the information from the documents provided and your knowledge of history, write a well-organized essay that includes an introduction, a body of several paragraphs, and a conclusion. Use examples from at least four documents in the body of the essay. Support your response with relevant facts, examples, and details. Include additional outside information.

GUIDELINES

In your essay, be sure to:

- Address all aspects of the **Task** by accurately analyzing and interpreting at least *four* documents.

- Incorporate information from the documents in the body of the essay.

- Incorporate relevant outside information.

- Support the theme with relevant facts, examples, and details.

- Use a logical and clear plan of organization.

- Introduce the theme by establishing a framework that is beyond a simple statement of the **Task** or **Historical Context**.

- Conclude the essay with a summation of the theme.

Activity 13 Reading Like a Historian

The Cold War in the Developing World

Part A: Using Source Materials

HISTORICAL CONTEXT Though it began as hostility between the United States and the Soviet Union, the Cold War had profound and lasting effects on countries around the world. As part of their conflict, the two superpowers intervened frequently in the affairs of developing countries in Asia, Africa, Latin America, and the Pacific.

TASK Using information from the documents and your knowledge of world history, answer the questions that follow each document in Part A. Your answers to the questions will help you write the Part B essay.

DIRECTIONS Examine the following documents and answer the short-answer questions that follow each document.

DOCUMENT 1

> **Sec. 620. Prohibitions Against Furnishing Assistance.**—(a)(1) No assistance shall be furnished under this Act to the present government of Cuba; nor shall any such assistance be furnished to any country which furnishes assistance to the present government of Cuba unless the President determines that such assistance is in the national interest of the United States. As an additional means of implementing and carrying into effect the policy of the preceding sentence, the President is authorized to establish and maintain a total embargo upon all trade between the United States and Cuba.
>
> —Foreign Assistance Act of 1961 (P.L. 87-195)

1. What activities were prohibited by this passage of the Foreign Assistance Act? Why do you think those activities were prohibited?

   _____

   _____

2. In 1961 Cuba had only recently come under the control of Fidel Castro and the Communist Party. What do you think the U.S. government hoped to achieve through the Foreign Assistance Act?

   _____

   _____

Activity 13

Reading Like a Historian

The Cold War in the Developing World

DOCUMENT 2
Effects of the Vietnam War

Before You View Between 1959 and 1975, Communist and democratic armies fought for control of Vietnam in Southeast Asia. Communist North Vietnam was aided by the Soviet Union and China, while South Vietnam was supported by the United States, Australia, New Zealand, and other democracies. Though the war was caused by political disputes, it wreaked havoc on the people and countryside of Vietnam, causing millions of dollars of damage and incalculable suffering. How does this political cartoon express those results?

"Let this session of Congress be known as the session—which declared all-out war on human poverty."
—PRESIDENT JOHNSON, JANUARY 8, 1964.

© Victor Weisz, Evening Standard, 12-1-1965, British Artist Cartoon Archive, University of Kent/Solo Syndication

3. What images are shown in this cartoon? Why do you think the artist chose those images?

   _____

   _____

4. What does the quote from President Johnson mean? Why is it included with the cartoon? Do you think it was originally used in this context?

   _____

   _____

Activity 13

Reading Like a Historian
The Cold War in the Developing World

DOCUMENT 3

Before You Read In December 1979 the Soviet Union sent troops into Afghanistan, largely in response to pro-American sentiments held by Afghan leader Hafizullah Amin. At the urging of Yuri Andropov, the head of the KGB—the Soviet intelligence agency—the Soviets replaced Amin with a Communist regime.

> In this extremely difficult situation, which has threatened the gains of the April revolution and the interests of maintaining our national security, it has become necessary to render additional military assistance to Afghanistan, especially since such requests had been made by the previous administration in DRA [Democratic Republic of Afghanistan]. In accordance with the provisions of the Soviet-Afghan treaty of 1978, a decision has been made to send the necessary contingent of the Soviet Army to Afghanistan. Riding the wave of patriotic sentiments that have engaged fairly large numbers of the Afghan population in connection with the deployment of Soviet forces which was carried out in strict accordance with the provisions of the Soviet-Afghan treaty of 1978, the forces opposing H. Amin organized an armed operation which resulted in the overthrow of H. Amin's regime. This operation has received broad support from the working masses, the intelligentsia, significant sections of the Afghan army, and the state apparatus, all of which welcomed the formation of a new administration of the DRA and the PDPA [People's Democratic Party of Afghanistan].
>
> —Yuri Andropov, Report to the Central Committee of the Communist Party of the Soviet Union, 1979

5. Why does Andropov say the Soviets invaded Afghanistan?

_____

_____

6. What effect do you think the Soviets hoped their intervention in Afghanistan would have on affairs in nearby countries?

_____

_____

Activity 13   Reading Like a Historian

The Cold War in the Developing World

DOCUMENT 4

Before You Read According to recently declassified documents published by the Central Intelligence Agency, some American officials supported the direct overthrow—or even the assassination—of Guatemalan president Jacobo Arbenz in the 1950s. In the end, Arbenz was overthrown by an alliance of Guatemalan exiles with secret aid supplied by the CIA.

As early as 1952 U.S. policymakers viewed the government of President Arbenz with some alarm. Although he had been popularly elected in 1950, growing Communist influence within his government gave rise to concern in the United States that Arbenz had established an effective working alliance with the Communists. Moreover, Arbenz' policies had damaged US business interests in Guatemala; a sweeping agrarian reform called for the expropriation and redistribution of the United Fruit Company's land. Although most high-level U.S. officials recognized that a hostile government in Guatemala by itself did not constitute a direct security threat to the United States, they viewed events there in the context of the growing global Cold War struggle with the Soviet Union and feared that Guatemala could become a client state from which the Soviets could project power and influence throughout the Western Hemisphere.

CIA and Intelligence Community reports tended to support the view that Guatemala and the Arbenz regime were rapidly falling under the sway of the Communists . . . the CIA assessment of the situation had support within the Truman administration as well. This led to the development of a covert action program designed to topple the Arbenz government— PBFORTUNE.

—Gerald K. Haines, CIA History Staff Analysis, 1995

---

7. According to this passage, what was PBFORTUNE? Why was it created?

_____

_____

8. What threat did the U.S. government think Guatemala posed to the West?

_____

_____

Activity 13

Reading Like a Historian

The Cold War in the Developing World

DOCUMENT 5

Before You Read In 1979 representatives from 95 countries around the world met in Havana, Cuba, for a summit meeting. Calling themselves the Non-Aligned Movement (NAM), these countries were meeting to express their independence from world power blocs such as NATO and the Warsaw Pact. The purpose of the NAM was to fight injustice and aggression by the world's superpowers, a purpose expressed by Cuban president Fidel Castro in this address to the United Nations.

> We are 95 countries from all the continents representing the vast majority of humanity. We are united by determination to defend cooperation among our countries, free national and social development, sovereignty, security, equality and self-determination. We are associated in the endeavor to change the current system of international relations based on injustice, inequality and oppression. We act on international policy as a global independent factor.
>
> Gathered in Havana, the movement has just reaffirmed its principles and confirmed its objectives. The nonaligned countries insist that it is necessary to eliminate the abysmal inequality that separates developed and developing countries. We therefore struggle to eliminate the poverty, hunger, disease and illiteracy that hundreds of millions of human beings are still experiencing.
>
> We want a new world order based on justice, equality, and peace to replace the unfair and unequal system that prevails today under which, according to the proclamation in the Havana declaration, wealth continues to be concentrated in the hands of a few powers whose economies, based on waste, are maintained thanks to the exploitation of workers and to the transfer and plundering of natural and other resources of countries in Africa, Latin America, and other regions of the world.
>
> —Fidel Castro, address to the United Nations, October 12, 1979

9. What does Castro say the NAM was founded to do?

_____

_____

10. How was the founding of the NAM a response to the Cold War?

_____

_____

Reading Like a Historian

Activity 13

Reading Like a Historian
The Cold War in the Developing World

Part B: Preparing an Oral Presentation

HISTORICAL CONTEXT Though it began as hostility between the United States and the Soviet Union, the Cold War had profound and lasting effects on countries around the world. As part of their conflict, the two superpowers intervened frequently in the affairs of developing countries in Asia, Africa, Latin America, and the Pacific.

TASK Using information from the documents and your knowledge of world history, prepare an oral presentation in which you:

- Explain the actions of the United States, the Soviet Union, and other major developed countries toward developing countries during the Cold War.

- Analyze the responses of developing countries to interference in their affairs by the superpowers.

DIRECTIONS Using the information from the documents provided and your knowledge of history, prepare a well-organized oral presentation that includes an introduction, a body, and a conclusion. Use examples from at least *four* documents in your presentation. Support your presentation with relevant facts, examples, and details. Include additional outside information.

GUIDELINES
In your presentation, be sure to:

- Address all aspects of the **Task** by accurately analyzing and interpreting at least *four* documents.

- Incorporate information from the documents in the body of the essay.

- Incorporate relevant outside information.

- Support the theme with relevant facts, examples, and details.

- Use a logical and clear plan of organization.

- Introduce the theme by establishing a framework that is beyond a simple statement of the **Task** or **Historical Context**.

- Conclude the presentation with a summation of the theme.

Activity 1: Religion in Ancient India

Part A

Possible answers:

1. The passage from the *Bhagavad Gita* describes, in broad outline, the class structure of the civilization out of which Hinduism arose.
2. There would be order in society. People would know what roles or duties they needed to fulfill.
3. Siddhartha is denying the class structure of society. He is saying that the group he was born into does not matter.
4. Buddhists might have used the Buddha's words to eliminate the division of society into classes.
5. The Buddha appears calm and serene. His form is fully human.
6. The statue's emphasis might reflect the Buddhist belief in the calmness and serenity of the Buddha as a model of humanity.
7. The statue depicts Siva with a humanlike face and humanlike legs.
8. Siva is shown with superhuman qualities, like four arms. Siva's pose perhaps seems superhuman.
9. The Buddha avatar and the Buddha statue are in similar poses. The Buddha avatar has non-human qualities that are not shown in the Buddha statue.
10. Hindus consider the Buddha to have godlike qualities. Perhaps Hindus were trying to prevent conversions to Buddhism by including the Buddha into the Hindu belief system.

Part B

Students' essays will vary. Students should recognize that Buddhism differs from Hinduism in its views toward the structure of society and in the fact that the religion's main figure, the Buddha, was human and not a god. The religions are similar in that Hindus accept many of the teachings of the Buddha and even consider him to be an incarnation of the Vishnu aspect of Brahman. Both religion's also arose in the same part of the world, and therefore reflect many similar influences.

Activity 2: Decline and Fall of the Roman Empire

Part A

Possible answers:

1. The wall may have been built to protect the Romans from whoever lived on the other side—to thwart an invasion.
2. That Hadrian's Wall was built suggests that there was conflict or tension between the Romans and their neighbors. It suggests that life was dangerous on the fringes of the Roman Empire.
3. The four figures are all equal and identical. None seems greater or more powerful than the others. Each tetrarch clutches a sword and wears a crown, which suggests that each has military powers in addition to political ones.
4. The Roman Empire had grown too large to be ruled over effectively by one person. The existence of four rulers would allow each ruler to focus his energies on a smaller area, leading to more effective government and staving off decline.
5. Diocletian attributes the rise in prices to the greed and wickedness of Roman merchants.
6. Rising prices could have led to increased poverty, which in turn could have led to revolts by dissatisfied citizens against the government.
7. The defeat is considered one of the worst in the history of the Roman Empire.
8. Details that suggest the Roman army was overwhelmed include its tumult and confusion, the infantry being exhausted by toil and danger, and the dense battalions of the enemy. This might indicate that the Roman army was on the brink of, or already in, a state of decline.
9. The author states that one effect of the inequities between Rome's rich and poor

Reading Like a Historian

citizens is that the poor would rather live with the barbarians than among the Romans.

10. The author says that for Rome's poor life among the barbarians is more just and fair than life among the Romans.

Part B

Answers will vary, but students should indicate in their essays that the Roman Empire was experiencing threats from outside forces, division inside the Empire, and discontent among its own citizens. Students should then describe how the effects of those challenges contributed to the fall of the Western Roman Empire.

Activity 3: Art of the Islamic World

Part A

Possible answers:

1. The pages include highly elaborate and decorative Arabic script as well as examples of geometric designs.
2. The development of calligraphy and illumination suggests that Muslims revere their scriptures and seek to celebrate and adorn them.
3. Arabesque features repeated patterns of interlocking shapes and figures and do not portray human or animal figures. The window is a repeated pattern of interlocking shapes. The window does not portray human or animal figures.
4. The arabesque style stresses order and structure, which would seem to reflect an appreciation for math.
5. The building is elaborately decorated because it was designed to praise Allah. The décor suggests that its builders were devout Muslims who wanted to impress viewers with their devotion.
6. The mosque incorporates calligraphy and the arabesque designs. The symmetry of the minarets reflects an appreciation for math.

7. The poet is addressing Allah and seeks to convey the poet's absolute devotion to him.
8. Poetry is a particularly suitable style for expressing an emotional message, such as the one conveyed by Rabi'ah al-Adawiyya.
9. The narrator gives the man money because he thinks the man is poor and hungry.
10. The story reflects the Islamic belief in showing compassion for the poor and less fortunate.

Part B

Students' multimedia presentations will vary. Presentations should reflect awareness of the major Islamic art forms of calligraphy and illumination, arabesque styles in art and architecture, and poetry and literature that is influenced by the faith of the writers and the culture of Islam.

Activity 4: Europe's Crusader Culture

Part A

Possible answers:

1. The passage describes the collection of money from people to help pay for the Crusades
2. Officials of the government are helping to collect the money.
3. Venice was an active and thriving city.
4. The city is on the water, which helps explain its position as a commercial center.
5. Both castles have rounded walls with tall towers and thick walls.
6. European rulers might fear attacks from their rivals or from invaders. Stronger castles could repel those attacks better than earlier designs.
7. On certain days, people cannot carry weapons or wear armor. Even on days when weapons were allowed, people were not allowed to fight.
8. Restrictions on fighting forced people to work together, which helped bring about

Reading Like a Historian

new ideas and a new period of creativity and prosperity.

9. Most of them are not to be trusted, though a few are admirable.

10. He has adopted many Muslim customs and changed his diet. He has also hired servants from the area.

Part B

Answers will vary, but students should recognize that the Crusades helped promote the growth of cities such as Venice, changed the technology of warfare, increased the power of the Church and governments, and produced far-reaching social changes. After the Crusades, Europe had increased contact with other parts of the world, was less violent internally, and was slightly more urban and commercial.

Activity 5: China during the Ming Dynasty

Part A

Possible answers:

1. He believes that following the way of Confucius is central to Chinese society.

2. They will prosper and succeed as individuals, and the state will prosper and succeed.

3. The size of the complex suggests that the emperor was powerful and wealthy.

4. The fact that the Ming dynasty could build such an elaborate structure suggests that they led a well-organized and highly developed society.

5. Elements of nature, such as the swan and flowers, were traditional in China's art.

6. The Ming era marked a return of Chinese rule, and there was a desire to reaffirm Chinese greatness.

7. The King feels that China's influence has been positive in a variety of ways.

8. The king feared China or wanted to please China and win its continued support.

9. Chinese manufacturing was fairly sophisticated.

10. The recording of this knowledge would spread the success and prosperity of the dynasty over a wider area.

Part B

Answers will vary, but students should recognize that the Ming era was marked by a return of traditional Chinese forms and ideas and an expansion of Chinese power. The dynasty marked an advance in Chinese government, power around the globe, and achievement in arts and sciences.

Activity 6: The Northern Renaissance

Part A

Possible answers:

1. Erasmus seems critical of this practice, suggesting that it is unethical, unreligious, and meant to enrich the dishonest.

2. He suggests that certain prayers, though not all, were written by unscrupulous men who taught people to use them almost as charms against evil, a practice that he finds neither helpful nor Christian.

3. Decorative details such as the chandelier, the mirror, the details of the clothing are realistically drawn. In addition, the people are presented as lifelike and not idealized as they would have been in some other periods.

4. The mirror provides a reflection of the couple, which both adds to the realism of the painting and suggests that it serves as a reflection of an actual event.

5. This fact suggests that people of the Northern Renaissance were finding meaning in the lives of ordinary, nonnoble people.

6. Brueghel seems to see beauty and meaning in recording what others might have considered unremarkable scenes.

7. The speaker praises the wide availability of knowledge and learning for even ordinary people.

8. Rabelais seems to be saying that access to education can give anyone, even the

Reading Like a Historian

lowliest members of society, power and influence in society. Education, not birth or divine guidance, is the key to success.

9. Don Quixote seems to be seeking glory and wealth and the favor of God.

10. The author sees Don Quixote as silly, perhaps deluded. His goals are trumped up, and his pride is excessive. By extension, he seems to be arguing that the whole system of chivalry was nothing but a meaningless façade.

Part B

Answers will vary, but students should recognize that the Northern Renaissance expanded on the earlier movement's fascination with detail and accurate depictions of the human form. It involved a deeper exploration of the concerns of "real" people, and it criticized the practices of such traditionally powerful institutions as the church and chivalry.

Activity 7: Impact of European Explorations Around the World

Part A

Possible answers:

1. The passage describes how African children—including the author and his sister—were commonly abducted from their home villages.

2. The passage suggests that Africans played the role of capturing people for sale into slavery, a fact that could have created deep conflict in the African world.

3. The letter states that the purposes were to serve God and make money.

4. When they learned of the trade, the Portuguese wanted to become involved so they could make large amounts of money. This led to increased European influence in India and probably in the reduction of that country's income.

5. The Inca ruler Atahualpa is realzing that the Spanish have allied with his enemies and that he is in danger.

6. By being divided among themselves, the Inca weakened their resistance to conquest, making it easier for the Spanish to take Peru.

7. The short-term effects include a sharp drop in population.

8. The loss of population made life much more difficult for those who survived. The weakened groups would be much less able to overcome various challenges or adversaries.

9. The Native Americans are riding on horses while hunting bison.

10. The horse allowed Native Americans a new way to hunt large game such as bison. It also provided a means of transportation with which groups could move over large distances and led to new tactics in war.

Part B

Answers will vary, but students' presentations should note how the arrival of Europeans brought change to Africa, Asia, and the Americas. It altered relationships among native peoples in places like Africa; it altered commercial relationships in Asia; and it altered political relationships and even the course of nature in the Americas, where disease and the introduction of horses devastated populations and changed ways of living.

Activity 8: The French Revolution

Part A

Possible answers:

1. The artist's comment is sarcastic and suggests that the artist considers the guillotine to be barbaric.

2. Yes; while his face is calm and peaceful, the scene around him is remarkably violent.

3. The tree and apples represent the outcomes of the French Revolution. This is clear from the words that appear on the trunk and on the apples, which allude to ideas or results of the French Revolution.

Reading Like a Historian

4. The tree and apples are in poor condition, which suggests the artist's negative view of the Revolution.

5. Jefferson considered their deaths to be similar to the deaths of soldiers who fall in a battle—tragic, but necessary to the larger cause.

6. According to Jefferson, the victims will be remembered for their sacrifice, which resulted in liberty.

7. The excesses of the French Revolution are a product of the terrible system that it sought to replace.

8. Shelley argues that the downtrodden people of France were not prepared to rule well because of their history of having been oppressed.

9. The fact that one rival is whipping the other suggests that a French invasion could cause fighting among the different groups in Great Britain similar to the fighting among the French during the Terror.

10. A Great Britain under French control would be chaotic and violent.

Part B

Answers will vary, but students should recognize that the French Revolution inspired differing views—some negative and some positive—among foreign observers. You may refer to the rubrics provided in the back of the book to analyze students' essays.

Activity 9: The Enlightenment Changes Views of Government

Part A

Possible answers:

1. Natural law stems from natural reason and was created by God.

2. The passage suggests that the authors do not favor absolute monarchy, because they believe in the equality of all people.

3. The goal is the glory of the state, which produces among the people a sense of liberty.

4. She suggests that monarchy can be consistent with good government and the fulfillment of the people provided it seeks the right goals.

5. Bolívar seems to be concerned about failing in his duties and being subject to the criticism of his countrymen.

6. Bolívar's views suggest the belief that leaders should be held accountable for their efforts by the people.

7. The idea of rights is illustrated through the perceived equality of all people in the image. The idea of liberty is suggested by the fact that Europeans and slaves are celebrating together.

8. The coat, which is being given to a slave, indicates the equality of all people. The sword and rifle on the ground represent freedom from violence and oppression.

9. The community is raising a liberty pole as part of a celebration.

10. The event seems to be a celebration. The involvement of the entire community suggests that people may have thought everyone deserved to take part in the government.

Part B

Answers will vary, but students should recognize the Enlightenment belief in the fundamental equality of all people and in the need for liberty. These beliefs caused monarchs to modify their views and goals, and it inspired independence movements in many places.

Activity 10: The Impact of Imperialism on Subject People

Part A

Possible answers:

1. The mining operations seem to have had little positive impact on the land or the communities. It employs local people, but it does not appear that there is a lot of wealth generated in the local community.

2. It likely produced great wealth for the British, for diamonds are very valuable. It appears to have produced little wealth among the local people.

3. The Boxers were angry about the impact of Christianity in China.

4. Christianity may have represented all western influences. It may have undermined other religions or cultures.

5. The arrival of the Americans is portrayed as a positive event that has brought prosperity and health.

6. The cartoon depicts the people of the countries shown as the recipient of benefits. This view is realistic in that there were likely some improvements under American colonial rule, but unrealistic in that they fail to show the extent to which America benefited at their colonies' expense.

7. Gandhi appears in humble clothing and in humble surroundings.

8. The spinning wheel was the Indians' means of producing cloth and clothing for themselves. It represented the Indian way of life before the British arrived.

9. Colonialism gave one group power over the other and heightened rivalries.

10. The unfairness and inequalities produced hard feelings that multiplied and grew deeper over time.

Part B

Answers will vary, but students should recognize that imperialism produced some positive and negative effects for the subject people, including economic effects, cultural effects, and the effects of nationalism.

Activity 11: The High Cost of World War I

Part A

Possible answers:

1. They wanted to ensure that all their partners remained in the fight, making their force stronger.

2. In that case, the Germans and their allies might have been able to isolate one or another of the Allies, force them out of the war, and thereby weaken the Allies.

3. They have developed more powerful explosives and bombs.

4. The nature of the trenches are such that no side will be able to completely defeat the other.

5. The destructive power of the modern artillery was extreme.

6. The picture suggests that few people or armies could really survive a barrage of the type shown. Large numbers of people would die in such an attack.

7. The old rules of warfare no longer apply.

8. War cannot be fought effectively under the old rules. The whole conception of what war is has changed.

9. The tank's armor, its guns, and its ability to move across a rough, bombed-out terrain and over trenches make it a promising weapon for the World War I battlefield.

10. The appearance of tanks will likely lead to the production of new, more powerful weapons to combat it.

Part B

Answers will vary, but students should recognize that World War I introduced some complex political situations—alliances that drew together several rich and powerful nations. It also introduced some new and improved technology. These helped create conditions in which there were large numbers of soldiers on the battlefield, committed to maintaining the fight in spite of the stalemate and in spite of the large amount of destruction.

Activity 12: How Did the Postwar Era Affect Population Groups?

Part A

Possible answers:

1. The Roma had much of their culture and their history destroyed during the war..

　　　　　　　　　　Reading Like a Historian

2. Their tradition was largely passed on orally, and the ability of the Roma to do that was damaged during the war.
3. He is concerned that relocating from one part of the world, particularly at a time when the world is still greatly disrupted by the effects of war, can be dangerous and difficult.
4. The creation of Israel may have represented a hope and a challenge to the Jews of Europe, and it might also have represented a break, possibly a welcome one, from their recent history.
5. The creation of Israel in the land of Palestine might have been a threat to the people living there.
6. Some Palestinians might have resented having their political fate dictated to them by an outside force. They may have resented losing what they viewed as their land to the Jewish State.
7. The Germans were forced to move with little preparation and with the few possessions they could transport.
8. The forced relocation must have been a terrible disruption to people and their communities.
9. He is upset because his people did not ask for partition, they see themselves as one people, and they need to be united in order to solve their problems.
10. He foresees the division of his country as a destructive blow to his people's ability to move forward and create a functioning society.

Part B

Answers will vary, but students should recognize that the defeated and victimized of World War II continued to face difficult adjustments and conditions after the war. The challenges included the need to rebuild cultures that had been attacked and destroyed, the need to relocate to new places; and the difficulties of the ongoing political disruptions and rivalries, such as those of the Cold War.

Activity 13: The Cold War in the Developing World

Part A

Possible answers:
1. The Act prohibited any U.S. aid to Cuba or to countries that gave aid to Cuba. It also set up a trade embargo against Cuba.
2. The United States hoped that the lack of financial assistance or trade with Cuba would weaken the Castro regime, leading to its fall and replacement.
3. The cartoon shows a presumably poor Vietnamese woman and her child, both looking unhappy and scared. It also shows an American plane dropping bombs behind them. The artist used these images to illustrate the effects of Western involvement in the Vietnam War on the people of that country.
4. Johnson meant that he and Congress would try to put an end to poverty. The artist used to quote to reinforce his point that the poor people of Vietnam are the ones suffering most from the war. This was obviously not the context in which Johnson meant the quote to be used.
5. Andropov says that recent events in Afghanistan threaten the Soviet Union's security and violated a treaty between the Soviet Union and Afghanistan.
6. The Soviets may have hoped that other countries would be swayed by the establishment of a Communist government in Afghanistan to become Communist themselves.
7. PBFORTUNE was a covert plan designed to overthrow the government of Guatemala, which had developed close ties to Communism.
8. The government feared that Guatemala would serve as a springboard for the introduction of Communist ideas in the Western Hemisphere.
9. Castro says the purpose of the NAM was to defend cooperation, development, independence, and security among its members.

Reading Like a Historian

10. The NAM was established in response to interference in developing countries by superpowers during the Cold War.

Part B

Answers will vary, but students should note that the United States and the Soviet Union both acted to protect their own interests by influencing the governments of developing countries. The United States worked to spread democracy and prevent the growth of Communism, while the Soviet Union tried to create new Communist governments. Students should also note that developing countries had little say in this interference, which led to resentment and the banding together of many countries to oppose the superpowers.

Reading Like a Historian

Rubric 1: Document-Based Essay

DIRECTIONS This form is designed to help you evaluate document-based essays. Read the statements below. Then indicate the number from the following scale that reflects your assessment of the student's work in each document-based essay.

1 = Weak   2 = Moderately Weak   3 = Average   4 = Moderately Strong   5 = Strong

1. The organization of the essay is clear and easy to follow.
   1   2   3   4   5

2. The essay incorporates relevant outside information.
   1   2   3   4   5

3. The essay accurately analyzes and interprets the required number of documents.
   1   2   3   4   5

4. The essay contains a clear thesis statement.
   1   2   3   4   5

5. Facts, examples, and details support the thesis statement.
   1   2   3   4   5

6. The essay establishes a framework that is beyond a simple restatement of the Task or Historical Context.
   1   2   3   4   5

7. The essay demonstrates an understanding of the topic and related concepts.
   1   2   3   4   5

8. The assignment is neatly typed or handwritten.
   1   2   3   4   5

9. The spelling, punctuation, and grammar on the writing assignment are accurate.
   1   2   3   4   5

10. Overall, the essay represents the writer's full potential.
    1   2   3   4   5

Additional Comments:

Total Points/Grade: _____

Rubric 2: Multimedia Presentation

DIRECTIONS This form is designed to help you evaluate student-created multimedia presentations. Read the statements below. Then indicate the number from the following scale that reflects your assessment of the student's or group's work.

1 = Weak   2 = Moderately Weak   3 = Average   4 = Moderately Strong   5 = Strong

1. The topic of the presentation meets the requirements of the assignment.
   1   2   3   4   5

2. The presentation appears to be well researched.
   1   2   3   4   5

3. The content of the presentation is accurate and appropriate.
   1   2   3   4   5

4. The presentation indicates an understanding of content.
   1   2   3   4   5

5. The presentation indicates an ability to synthesize information.
   1   2   3   4   5

6. The presentation includes the required number of elements.
   1   2   3   4   5

7. The presentation is neatly executed and inviting.
   1   2   3   4   5

8. The presentation makes good technical use of the capabilities of multimedia.
   1   2   3   4   5

9. If a group project, each group member appears to have participated in the development of the presentation.
   1   2   3   4   5

10. Overall, the presentation represents the individual's or group's full potential.
   1   2   3   4   5

Additional Comments:

Total Points/Grade: _____

Rubric 3: Oral Presentation

DIRECTIONS This form is designed to help you evaluate oral presentations. Read the statements below. Then indicate the number from the following scale that reflects your assessment of the student's work.

1 = Weak   2 = Moderately Weak   3 = Average   4 = Moderately Strong   5 = Strong

1. The topic of the presentation meets the requirements of the assignment.
   1   2   3   4   5

2. The presentation appears to be well researched.
   1   2   3   4   5

3. The presentation is well organized and cohesive.
   1   2   3   4   5

4. The presenter is adequately prepared for the presentation.
   1   2   3   4   5

5. The presentation indicated an understanding of the topic presented.
   1   2   3   4   5

6. The presenter employs a speaking and delivery style appropriate to the presentation topic.
   1   2   3   4   5

7. The presenter delivers ideas in a clear and concise fashion, without too much reliance on notes.
   1   2   3   4   5

8. The presenter speaks loudly and clearly enough to be heard by the audience.
   1   2   3   4   5

9. The presenter maintains eye contact with the audience.
   1   2   3   4   5

10. Overall, the work represents the presenter's full potential.
    1   2   3   4   5

Additional Comments:

Total Points/Grade: _____